SAMUEL BECKETT: A STUDY OF HIS NOVELS

EUGENE WEBB

SAMUEL BECKETT

A Study of His Novels

UNIVERSITY OF WASHINGTON PRESS

Seattle and London

Published by the University of Washington Press

Library of Congress Catalog Card Number 73-103289

Printed in Great Britain

For my Mother and Father

PREFACE

Looked at collectively, the works of Samuel Beckett reveal a remarkable continuity of theme. Together, his various writings constitute
a single, coherent presentation of a particular view of life. Beckett's
novels, especially, demand to be read as though each were a con-
stituent part of a larger whole. Of course, Beckett did not sit down
to write *More Pricks than Kicks* or *Murphy* with the idea that he
was eventually going to follow these works with *Watt*, the trilogy,
and *How It Is*, but as his career has proceeded he must have come
to see an important thematic continuity running through all of these
novels; and from *Watt* on he has deliberately connected each of
them by means of frequent allusions from one to another.

This explicit interrelatedness of Beckett's novels does not make
them easy to read. In fact, the author practically insists that if you
wish to read one of his novels, you should read them all in order
really to understand what he is trying to say. To some readers this
demand might seem unreasonable, perhaps even pretentious. 'A
neo-classicism,' John Updike called it, 'in which one's early works
are taken as the classics.'[1] To a reader who has become interested
enough in Beckett to read all, or at least several, of his novels,
however, the continuities that connect them make them, though
more demanding, more rewarding as well. Through a variety of
narrators, characters, and stories, Beckett has been able to make
in the total corpus of his novels a far more comprehensive portrait
of man in his relationship to the universe than he could have in
a single book. It is for the purpose of guiding the reader through
the intricacies of Beckett's novels to an understanding of their
over-all vision that the present study has been written.

Whereas several previous studies of Beckett have given a great
deal of attention to his use of comic techniques, the present study
concentrates on the development of his themes and his artistic
presentation of them. I do hope, however, that a reader approaching

Beckett for the first time will not be misled by my emphasis on Beckett's thought into reading him as primarily a solemn and somber philosopher. Although Beckett presents an unusually bleak assessment of man and of the human condition, he is actually a tremendously funny writer, perhaps the greatest comedian of the grotesque that literature has ever seen. It is precisely this combination of seriousness and humor that make Beckett so fascinating and so important. There is a kind of sublimity in a writer's being able to face with such honesty and courage a vision of life so pessimistic while at the same time retaining the inner freedom that enables him to laugh and to create.

Since this study is intended as a guidebook which should lead the reader to a more careful examination of Beckett himself, I have provided all important quotations with page numbers. These follow the quotations in parentheses, or in the case of several quotations from a single page, they follow the first quotation. The English language texts referred to are, with two exceptions, the editions published in New York by Grove Press. In the case of the trilogy, which has been published in a single volume as well as in a series of three separate volumes, my references are to the three separate volumes. The exceptions referred to above are *More Pricks than Kicks*, which was published in London by Chatto and Windus in 1934 and which has not been reissued, and *No's Knife*, a collection of Beckett's short fiction published in London by Calder and Boyars. References to the French texts are to the editions published by Éditions de Minuit, Paris. Further details on the editions cited from will, of course, be provided in the footnotes to the main body of this study. Publication data on the British editions of Beckett's works will be found in the Bibliography. Except for translations by Beckett and some others of his work, all translations are my own unless otherwise indicated.

I would like to express my appreciation to Professor William York Tindall of Columbia University for his careful reading of a part of this book and for his many helpful suggestions on it. I am also indebted to Professor Leon Roudiez of the same university for similar helpful criticism. I would also like to express my gratitude to my wife, Marilyn, for her help in the laborious task of proof reading this book. Final responsibility for any errors, either textual or interpretive, is, of course, my own.

ACKNOWLEDGMENTS

Passages from the following works of Samuel Beckett are quoted by permission of The Grove Press, Inc.: *Poems in English* (copyright © 1961 by Samuel Beckett), *Malone Dies* (copyright © 1956 by Grove Press), *The Unnamable* (copyright © 1958 by Grove Press), *How It Is* (copyright © 1964 by Grove Press), *Stories and Texts for nothing* (copyright © 1967 by Samuel Beckett), *Murphy, Proust, Watt,* and *Molloy* (published by Grove Press). Beckett's publishers in Great Britain, Calder and Boyars, Ltd., have also granted permission to quote from the above works as well as from *No's Knife* (first published in Great Britain, 1967, by Calder and Boyars, Ltd.). Passages from *More Pricks than Kicks* (copyright © 1934 by Chatto and Windus) are quoted by permission of Chatto and Windus, Ltd. Passages in French from the following works of Samuel Beckett are quoted by permission of Les Éditions de Minuit, Paris: *Molloy* (copyright © 1951 by Les Éditions de Minuit), *Malone meurt* (copyright © 1951 by Les Éditions de Minuit), *L'Innommable* (copyright © 1953 by Les Éditions de Minuit), *Nouvelle et Textes pour rien* (copyright © 1958 by Les Éditions de Minuit), and *Comment c'est* (copyright © 1961 by Les Éditions de Minuit). Passages from the article 'Moody Man of Letters' by Israel Shenker (copyright © 1956 by The New York Times Company. Reprinted by permission) are quoted by permission of The New York Times Company and of Mr Israel Shenker. Passages from Tom F. Driver, 'Beckett by the Madeleine' (*Columbia University Forum*, Summer 1961), are quoted by permission of the author and his agents, James Brown Associates. The passage from John Updike, 'How How It Is Was' (*New Yorker*, December 19, 1964), is quoted by permission of *The New Yorker*.

CONTENTS

SAMUEL BECKETT: A STUDY OF HIS NOVELS

CHAPTER I

Introduction: Beckett and the Twentieth Century

Samuel Barclay Beckett was born in 1906 of a middle-class Pro-
testant family at Foxrock near Dublin. In 1927 he received his
B.A. in Modern Literature from Dublin's Trinity College. Not long
after this he left Ireland to take a two-year position as *lecteur
d'anglais* at the École Normale Supérieure in Paris. Most of his
subsequent life was to be spent in France. Immediately he entered
into the life of the colony of literary and artistic expatriates from
all over Europe who congregated in Paris at the time. One of the
most prominent members of this group was Beckett's fellow country-
man, James Joyce, who was already famous for his *Ulysses* and
whose *Finnegans Wake* was in progress. Beckett's knowledge of
French, later to become his main literary language, must have been
impressive even at that time, because Joyce engaged him in 1930
as the principal translator for the French version of *Anna Livia
Plurabelle*. This began a close association between Beckett and
Joyce which lasted as long as Joyce lived.

It has been assumed by some that since Beckett spent a great
deal of time with Joyce he must have held the formal position of
secretary to him.[1] Actually, the relationship was more informal,
part friendship and perhaps part hero worship. On a few occasions
Beckett took down passages of *Finnegans Wake* as Joyce dictated,
but this was out of friendship on Beckett's part rather than because
he was formally engaged for this sort of work. Richard Ellmann
recounts an amusing anecdote told him by Beckett about one such
session of dictation. During the dictation there was a knock on
the door. Joyce said, 'Come in.' Beckett had not noticed the knock,

so he put Joyce's words down in the text. When Joyce found out later, he said, 'Let it stand.' Beckett told Ellmann he felt 'fascinated and thwarted' by this method of writing.[2]

Certainly Beckett's relationship with Joyce was important to him, and perhaps to Joyce as well, although it is difficult to determine exactly what it meant to either. Peggy Guggenheim said she thought Joyce loved Beckett as a son.[3] Perhaps, but according to Ellmann, Joyce also kept Beckett at a distance. As Ellmann described it, the friendship was as unique as were its two partici- pants : both were taciturn, and their conversations were often made up largely of long silences directed toward each other.[4]

The influence of Joyce's art on Beckett's has been greatly over- estimated by those critics who have described Beckett as an out- dated imitation of Joyce.[5] The two writers are really very different : Joyce constructed in his works a tightly organized universe in which each detail was suffused with symbolic import; Beckett's novels are more loosely constructed, less systematic.

This is not to say, however, that Beckett did not owe much to Joyce. He did. In his essay on Joyce in *Our Exagmination* Beckett praised the manner in which Joyce had shown how to unite form and content : 'His writing is not *about* something; *it is that some- thing itself.*'[6] Although Beckett's method of uniting form and content in his own works was not to be the same as Joyce's, he has also been concerned with trying to find forms that would adequately express his vision. As he told Tom F. Driver in an interview, 'there will be new form, and . . . this form will be of such a type that it admits the chaos and does not try to say that the chaos is really something else. . . . To find a form that accommodates the mess, that is the task of the artist now.'[7] The important difference between Beckett and Joyce lies in this attempt to accommodate form to chaos. Although Joyce had lost his faith in his religious tradition, he constructed an aesthetic form in his novels and stories that attempted to reimpose the lost pattern of meaning on a universe that would have seemed meaningless to him without man's ability to interpret it in human terms. Beckett would probably consider Joyce one of those who try to make it appear 'that the chaos is really something else.'[8]

Beckett probably owes more to Joyce in the area of language. Joyce had used and made fashionable a colourful, colloquial lan- guage, rich in play on words. Beckett's first collection of stories,

More Pricks than Kicks, is virtually overburdened with linguistic brilliance. When Belacqua Shuah, the central character of all the stories, is doing something as simple as making himself a sandwich, for example, the narrator heaps his description with figurative language : 'He clapped the toasted rounds together, he brought them smartly together like cymbals, they clave the one to the other on the viscid salve of Savora.'[9] In many places the language is so florid that the meaning is difficult to follow. Beckett himself may have decided these verbal displays were excessive since he has never had the volume reprinted,[10] which is unfortunate as it is actually an enjoyable and, for anyone concerned with Beckett's development as a writer, a significant work.

Beckett's next volume was the novel *Murphy*, which appeared in 1938. Here he still reminds one of Joyce, at least in language. In *Watt*, on the other hand, which was written during the German Occupation, from 1942 to 1944,[11] he began to search for a form and language uniquely his own with which to convey his vision of an empty universe in which man's thoughts are at best irrelevant. As his own disillusionment with human systems of thought became more despairing, he saw language, the vehicle of thought, not as a game, as it had seemed in *More Pricks than Kicks* and *Murphy*, but as a burden. Belacqua Shuah had thumbed his nose at life by his mock-heroic description of his sandwich, but Watt has to grope laboriously for the words with which to express his vision of the unintelligible.

Much of the atmosphere of *Watt* seems to have come from Kafka.[12] *Watt* bears considerable resemblance to *The Castle*. In both books the protagonists desire to see a certain enigmatic figure. Knott's house corresponds approximately to the Count's castle, though Watt really does gain entry to the house, whereas K. never enters the castle. Both Knott and the Count suggest something more than man, God perhaps, and both change shapes, suggesting that they lack a definable nature. The significant difference between *Watt* and *The Castle* is that while both Knott and the Count seem to be deity figures, the Count represents God in the sense of an ultimate authority, and Knott represents the Absolute, that which understood would render all intelligible. Knott's continual changing of shapes signifies that nothing is intelligible because there is a basic absurdity at the heart of the universe.

Beckett probably used Kafka again to a certain extent in the trilogy.[13] Youdi's organization with its agents and messengers is similar to the system of authority in the Count's castle. Both Youdi and the Count are unapproachably remote and consequently seem godlike to Moran and K. The parallel, however, would seem to end here. The remainder of the trilogy, after Moran's section, is hardly Kafkaesque. The style and the whole atmosphere are uniquely Beckett's.

Perhaps a more important twentieth-century influence on the trilogy than Kafka can be seen in the thought of certain existentialist philosophers with whom Beckett was undoubtedly familiar by the time the trilogy was being written in the late 1940's. The comfort Moran and Gaber take in the fact that, since they are members of a vast organization, their troubles are shared sounds like what Heidegger, in *Sein und Zeit,* would have called a flight to *das Man.* And in Moran's statement, 'I was a solid in the midst of other solids' (*Molloy,* p. 147), Beckett is probably alluding to Sartre's concept of the *en soi.* In Heidegger's interpretation, the flight to *das Man* is an attempt to avoid recognizing one's own individuality and freedom by giving up one's personal identity to an impersonal group. Sartre described the same type of self-deception from another point of view : a person can never cease to possess individual freedom, but he tries to convince himself he is not free by deceiving himself into believing he has a fixed essence which limits his freedom, that he is a definite 'thing,' what Sartre calls an '*en-soi.*' Although Beckett often parodies philosophical ideas in the tradition of 'learned wit,'[14] this seems to be a serious use of Sartre and Heidegger rather than a parody. Moran really was, at the time he is describing in this passage, a bourgeois who shared what Sartre believes to be a state of self-deception especially characteristic of the bourgeoisie. Beckett's trilogy as a whole, however, cannot really be described as an existentialist work; the characters move from certain illusions to a kind of disillusionment, but this is not represented as progress toward an existentialist freedom. The disillusionment in this case is by its very nature incomplete, as we shall see, and its end is not freedom but despair.

Beckett probably also draws on the tradition of the underground man as exemplified in such works as Dostoievsky's *Notes from the Underground* and Gogol's *The Diary of a Madman* in the nineteenth century and Kafka's *The Burrow* in the twentieth. Like the traditional underground man, the characters of Beckett's trilogy feel isolated from society and suffer from divided states of mind, and they also seek by techniques of irony to draw the reader into identification with them.[15]

One of the most intriguing features of Beckett's career as a writer has been his shift from the English language to French. The shift took place in the mid-1940's after Beckett had already completed a number of important works in English, and libraries still seem to be having some difficulty deciding whether he should be filed under French literature or under English. It has often been suggested that Beckett's reason for turning to French for a literary language after *Watt* may have been to free himself from the influence of Joyce's English.[16] This may be true. Beckett told one person that he changed to French *'parce qu'en français c'est plus facile d'écrire sans style.'*[17] There may also have been other reasons for the shift to French.[18] Since Beckett has never, except in fragmentary utterances, discussed his reasons for the change of language, all possible explanations must remain speculative. It may be that even he himself has no definite idea why he changed. To Israel Shenker, Beckett is reported to have said, 'It was more exciting for me—writing in French.'[19] Perhaps Beckett was motivated in part by the challenge to see what he could do with a language in which he had so steeped himself that it had practically become his own. Certainly his works in French show a skill that many native French writers could envy.

Skillful as he is with language, however, for Beckett language is less important than thought. Most of the changes that have taken place in Beckett's language from the time of *More Pricks than Kicks* to that of *How It Is* have been for the sake of more adequately conforming his expression to his thought. It is ironic that a writer for whom thought is so important should have as his message the untrustworthiness of human intelligence or of any meaningful pattern the human mind might think it can discover in the universe. Beckett told Tom Driver, 'I am not a philosopher.'[20] He probably meant that he held no allegiance to any system of thought, equally distrusting them all. But he is a thinker, and if a person whose entire body of work is a sort of prolegomenon to any future philosophy can be considered a philosopher, then Beckett is precisely that, at least in the sense that he is a man who has explored the limits of thought.

Although the development of Beckett's philosophical and artistic

vision has undoubtedly been influenced to greater or lesser extents
by the various twentieth-century figures discussed in this chapter,
the characteristic direction of his thought was already established
before he ever came into contact with most of them. The next
chapter will examine the early influence on him, during his
academic years, of writers representing a large range of the thought
of the past.

CHAPTER II

Early Writings: The First Statements of Beckett's Themes

One reason that Beckett's works show such a remarkable continuity of theme is that his characteristic view of life seems to have been formed very early in his career. Even his earliest writings reveal preoccupations with the same problems that he examines in his later works. Beckett's basic subject has been, from the very beginning, the difficulties of twentieth-century man in his efforts to understand his place in the universe. In his writings at least, Beckett shows little interest in the problems of society. Beckettian man's concern is primarily metaphysical. He is disillusioned with the hopes previous generations have had for ameliorating their lives by making changes in the world around them, and he is also disillusioned with all of the religious systems or metaphysical theories that previous generations have used to enable themselves to feel more or less at home in the universe. Beckett's career began with an examination of some of these previous systems and theories, and his writings as a whole can be read as, in part, an extended commentary on the inadequacies of these systems of thought.

Originally, Beckett intended to take up an academic career, and in fact he was well on his way to a distinguished position in the academic world when, in December, 1931, he quit his post as lecturer in French and assistant to the professor of Romance languages at Trinity College, Dublin, in order to devote himself entirely to creative writing. His academic background provided him with a considerable knowledge of intellectual history. Three figures in particular who interested him keenly during that period have played important roles in his later thought : Dante, Descartes, and Proust.

Together, these three thinkers represent for Beckett the intellectual background of the modern world, three successive phases through which Western man has passed. Dante represents the old, orderly world view with which modern man has necessarily become disillusioned. In its time, the medieval world view presented in *The Divine Comedy* offered man the picture of a purposeful life in a coherent, intelligible universe. Dante, following his mentor Aquinas, believed in a universal order embracing both the natural and the supernatural. This order was believed to have been established by a reliable, basically predictable God : God could not will evil because this would be contrary to His nature. Man's good was thought to correspond exactly with the good as understood and willed by God.

The good willed by Dante's God applied to both the natural and the supernatural aspects of man's life. God willed that men choose heaven, their supernatural good, but He was also concerned with the good in man's temporal life. He willed that men establish in the temporal world a natural political order that would correspond to the supernatural order of paradise. This would consist, maintained Dante, of a single universal empire in harmony with, but independent of, a single universal church. Dante's purpose in the *Commedia* was to interpret the divine plan both in its natural and in its supernatural aspects for his contemporaries. It was a plan which they could understand and which could and, for many, did give a sense of purpose to their lives; they could feel that in both their religious and their social lives they were serving the ultimate purposes of the universe.

Dante's metaphysics, the Aristotelian metaphysics he derived from Aquinas, was what might be called 'unitary' (as compared with 'dualistic'). The essential harmony between the natural and the supernatural applied within men as individuals, just as it did in society as a whole. A man's body and soul formed a single unit, and their goals were in harmony. The moral order as appointed by God could be discerned by man's reason and, with the help of grace, pursued by man's will. The moral life was believed to lead to felicity in this world and beatitude in the next. The good of the whole man was the good of both body and soul. In fact, from this point of view, the body and the soul were seen as so closely united that the one could hardly have any real existence apart from the other. In Canto XXV of the *Purgatorio*, for example, the spirit of Statius explains to Dante that the souls of the dead, while waiting for the return of their original bodies at the final resurrection, form interim bodies for themselves, complete with all the organs of sense, by impressing themselves upon the air. In Dante's world, the soul is at home in the body, and man is at home in the universe.

In Beckett's world, the situation is quite the opposite. There is no God and no universal order. Beckettian man does not feel at home in the universe, nor can he feel that any worldly goal serves any ultimate purpose. Man can find no intelligible pattern in the universe or in his own life. If man is honest, as some of Beckett's characters try to be, he must face this situation. But this is not a situation in which anyone, not even Beckett's most lucid characters, such as Molloy or the Unnamable, can easily acquiesce. His less lucid characters—Murphy and Moran are examples— try by various kinds of self-deception to retain their belief in at least some of the elements of the older world view. To a large extent Beckett's novels make up an extended commentary both on the untruth of Dante's religious and metaphysical system and on the inability of twentieth-century man to completely free himself of a tendency to want to see in the universe some of the order that Dante's beliefs seemed to give it.

More Pricks than Kicks and *Murphy* can both be read as, in part at least, commentaries on Dante's *Purgatorio*. The main character of *More Pricks than Kicks* is Belaqua Shuah, named after one of the characters in Dante's antepurgatory (*Purgatorio*, IV), the region in which the spiritually indolent, who delayed their repentance until the last possible moment, are required to spend a period of time equal to that which they wasted while on earth. Like his namesake in Dante, Beckett's Belacqua is said to be 'sinfully indolent,' and his goal in life is to protect and maintain his state of indolence. Both Murphy and Belacqua would like to escape from the burdens of life and thought into a condition of total inaction, a condition resembling that of the spirits in Dante's antepurgatory. Murphy even names one of the stages on the path to absolute freedom 'the Belacqua bliss.' Both men are deluded, however. From Beckett's point of view, there can be no permanent escape from the conditions of this existence.

In his later work this is shown clearly—in *The Unnamable*, for example. Because they still live with the illusion that life can have a goal, life for Murphy and Belacqua can appear to be purgatorial, that is, it can appear to be leading through a process of training or detachment to a kind of peace. Murphy is virtually following a spiritual discipline to purify himself of all that would tie him to his world. Both characters are objects of irony for the author, who knows that the hope of purgation and escape is a delusion.

Watt,[1] in this schema, serves as a parody of the *Paradiso*. Watt, traveling to Knott's house and finally ascending to the vision of Knott after labors that train his will to quietude, resembles Dante in his ascent through purgatory and paradise to the vision of God. Like Dante's God circled by nine orders of angels, Knott is always surrounded by his servants, 'in tireless assiduity turning . . . eternally turning about Mr Knott in tireless love' (*Watt*, pp. 61-62). Knott, however, is not Dante's God, not the God that Mr Spiro and others talk about at the beginning of the book, the God who is traditionally supposed to be eternal and immutable. Mr Knott changes shape constantly. If he is a type of God at all, it is the phenomenological God, the changing image of God that is all men have to live with in Beckett's universe. Watt is a man in quest of certainty, of knowledge of immutable truth. In Knott's house he learns that there can be no absolute knowledge of any kind. But even after learning this, he still cannot help continuing to try to understand the world around him : '. . . he was for ever falling into this old error, this error of the old days when, lacerated with curiosity, in the midst of substance shadowy he stumbled' (*Watt*, p. 227). Watt has learned that there is no absolute and no intelligible meaning in life, but, like all men, and like all Beckett's characters, he can never completely free himself from the need to go on looking for them. It is this necessity to keep on and on making the same mistakes that makes the reality of life a hell.

Paradise and purgatory are both delusions that Beckett's earlier works examine ironically and dismiss. The reality underlying all of the novels is hell. The trilogy and *How It Is* are explorations of this reality. In Beckett's work they occupy a position corresponding approximately to that of the *Inferno* in Dante's. Hell in Christian tradition is supposed to be primarily the absence of God.

In *Watt*, Beckett showed the emptiness of the idea of God. In the remaining novels he shows a total absence of God, an absence beyond anything that Dante could possibly have imagined. Dante's damned may be deprived of the direct vision of God, but they still know Him indirectly, that is, they know that He exists, and this knowledge makes the universe and their place in it at least partially intelligible to them. The suffering may not be any less painful for their knowledge of its justice, but at least they are not, like Beckett's characters, 'lacerated with curiosity' as to what it all means. The denizens of Beckett's Inferno have not even the comfort of knowing they are damned. Moran, at the beginning of his quest, thinks he understands something of what life is all about, but Molloy, Malone, the Unnamable, and the narrator of *How It Is* are in utter confusion. They cannot even satisfy themselves with the atheist's explanation that it is all meaningless. Just as they are compelled by an inexplicable inner necessity to keep moving across their bleak landscapes or through an infinity of mud, they are also compelled to keep trying to figure out an explanation for their fate. In *More Pricks than Kicks* and *Murphy*, insanity and death still seemed to the protagonists to offer means of escape from the necessity to go on thinking and trying to understand the unintelligible. *Watt* did not look for death, but he did go insane—his story is told by another inmate of the asylum— and insanity gave him no relief. The trilogy and *How It Is* rule out death in order to explore what man's condition would be if neither escape of any kind nor hope of escape were possible. Purgatory could have an exit, but hell cannot.

Cultural histories of the Western world have long interpreted Descartes as the thinker who marks the dividing point between the medieval and the modern world views. Although recent studies have shown both how dependent Descartes was on the philosophical concepts of the Middle Ages and how much more philosophically radical than Descartes were some of the scholastics themselves, William of Ockham and Nicholas of Autrecourt, for example, Descartes remains a convenient symbol of the breakup of the unitary world view of Aquinas and Dante. More than any previous thinker of the later Middle Ages or early Renaissance, Descartes stressed the metaphysical and epistemological problems involved in any attempt to connect the realm of spirit with the realm of matter. The composite of body and soul in a single substance that was described by the Thomistic system split apart for Descartes and his followers into a body and a soul, the connection between which was highly problematical. Some of Descartes's followers, such as Malebranche and Geulincx, separated the two even more radically than he. Geulincx's occasionalism interpreted spirit and matter as two parallel but totally unconnected systems. To explain how a person's mental impressions of the physical world could correspond to its reality, Geulincx used the analogy of two clocks, one representing matter, the other spirit, both wound up and set by the master clockmaker to run perfectly synchronously. From the occasionalist point of view, there could be no connection between the mental impression of a flash, for example, and the physical reality of an explosion, other than that both took place simultaneously.

Nevertheless, the occasionalists, by their assumption that God would make the two systems of matter and spirit parallel and synchronous, reveal their attachment to the old certainties. And Descartes did not wish to go even as far as they in breaking up the unity of man's world and of his being. Although he maintained that the body and soul were distinct and independent of each other, he also believed, for no reason that he was ever able to describe adequately; that information about the realm of matter passed in some mysterious manner through the physical senses to the spiritual mind.[2] Since his philosophy could provide no explanation for this connection between body and soul, his reasons for continuing to believe in it were probably emotional.

Beckett acquired a thorough knowledge of Descartes, both of his break with the past and of his ties to it, in the process of writing his Master's thesis on Descartes for Trinity College. One of Beckett's first published works, *Whoroscope* (1930), awarded a ten-pound prize for the best poem on the subject of time in a competition sponsored by Nancy Cunard, is a portrait of Descartes. It presents Descartes's stream-of-consciousness as he waits for his morning omelette, which, Beckett says in his probably facetiously elaborate *Waste Land* – like notes to the poem, the philosopher liked 'made of eggs hatched from eight to ten days.' As he waits, thinking of the passage of time and how it will inevitably lead him to death —'horoscope' means 'hour-watcher'—Descartes's passing thoughts and comments reveal how attached he really is to the world view of the Middle Ages. Although he swears 'by the brothers Boot'— who, according to Beckett's note, 'in 1640 refuted Aristotle in

Dublin'—he curses Galileo as a 'vile old Copernican lead-swinging son of a sutler' for saying that the earth is in motion. On the subject of reconciling his dualism with the Church's dogma of transubstantiation in the Eucharist, he insists that he believes whole-heartedly in transubstantiation and in Dante's 'great high bright rose,' the mystical body of Christ as imaged in the last cantos of the *Paradiso*.

Beckett makes numerous allusions to the ideas of Descartes and the occasionalists in his novels. In *More Pricks than Kicks*, Belacqua scoffs 'at the idea of a sequitur from his body to his mind' (p. 32). Murphy, more of a thinker than Belacqua, is fond of quoting 'the beautiful Belgo-Latin of Arnold Geulincx' to himself and has developed a fairly elaborate analysis of his mental life on the basis of Cartesian dualism :

> Murphy felt himself split in two, a body and a mind. They had intercourse apparently, otherwise he could not have known that they had anything in common. But he felt his mind to be bodytight and did not understand through what channel the intercourse was effected nor how the two experiences came to overlap [*Murphy*, p. 109].

To Murphy, as to the others among Beckett's characters who think in Cartesian terms,[3] the appeal of Cartesian dualism is that it seems to account for the intractability of the physical world and to offer an alternative to life in it. Without exception, Beckett's characters are physically tormented by their own decrepitude and by their inability to make life in any way physically comfortable for themselves. If the physical and mental realms of being can be interpreted as completely separate, then it would seem possible to escape from the frustration and pain of physical existence into the freedom of a purely mental existence. As the more lucid characters of the later works realize, however, this is an illusory hope.

Beckett is not a Cartesian. His works are based on a belief in the fundamental disharmony between body and mind, but they also show the futility and naïveté of imagining the mental world to be any less intractable than the physical. Beckett sees the world and man not as dualistic but as fragmentary. The conflict within man is not nearly so simple as a mere conflict between body and soul; it is a general disunity involving a multiplicity of conflicting physical and psychological impulses. Just as the Descartes of *Whoroscope* had one foot in the modern world and one foot in the medieval, so Cartesianism, though it helped break down belief in the Thomistic system, is still a system itself, and in Beckett's world reality is stubbornly resistant to all systems. The allusions to Dante and Descartes that run through Beckett's novels show both the world out of which twentieth-century man has grown and the manner in which he continues to cling to the comfort of the old illusions.

Of the three thinkers—Dante, Descartes, and Proust—who interested Beckett in his academic days and who seem to have become symbols to him of the stages in the cultural history of modern man, the one whose thought is most congenial to Beckett's own is the twentieth-century figure, Marcel Proust. Much of what Beckett has to say about Proust's ideas in his book, *Proust* (1931),[4] written as a scholarly monograph to further his intended academic career, may be interpreted as a description of what Beckett's own ideas either were at the time or were to become.

Beckett opens his study by announcing that he will discuss the role in Proust's thought of 'that double-headed monster of damnation and salvation—Time.' If Beckett had been speaking of what his own views were to become, he might have called time a monster of damnation and *apparent* salvation. Beckett's pessimism has less room for hope than Proust's. For Proust, as for Beckett, life in the temporal world, except when one's awareness of it is deadened by habit—'Habit is a great deadener,' says Didi in *Waiting for Godot*—is largely painful. The reason time is a 'monster of damnation' is that it erodes the insulation that patterns of habit can temporarily establish. In so far as the direct perception of reality would be painful, habit shields one from pain. When reality is beautiful, on the other hand—and for Proust, unlike Beckett, it often is—habit prevents the possibility of the joy that would constitute salvation. A person's self at any given moment is made up of the habits that govern him at that particular time. But no set of habits lasts forever, and no set of habits is adequate to shield one from reality in all circumstances. Therefore, life in time consists of what Beckett calls 'the perpetual exfoliation of personality' (*Proust*, p. 13): one set of habits must die in order that a new set may form to replace it. Beckett cites Marcel's first nights in the Grand Hotel at Balbec as an example. One set of habits had adapted him to sleeping in his own bedroom at home, but that made it all the more difficult for him to adapt to his new surroundings : 'Habit has not had time to silence the explosions of the clock, reduce the hostility of the violet curtains, remove the furniture and lower the inaccessible vault of this belvedere' (pp. 12-13). During the transition from one set of habits to another, the insulation of the old set breaks down before the new set is able to form. The result is an excruciating exposure to raw reality. Life tends to alternate between the boredom of habit and the pain of immediacy.

Beckett explains these features of Proust's thought very clearly, but for a reader more interested in Beckett himself than in what he has to say about Proust, his explanation only leads to further questions. It is true that, as Proust describes it, life, in the moments of direct perception of reality, tends much of the time to be painful, but why does Proust describe it in this way, and why does Beckett find Proust's view of life so interesting? One reason Proust, and his narrator Marcel, found reality painful is that Proust himself suffered from an acute asthmatic condition. Most people would find the transition from one set of habits or adaptations to another somewhat, though not extremely, uncomfortable, but Proust's reactions were more highly sensitive than those of most people. Another reason reality is presented in Proust's work as so painful, is that it is so illogical and uncontrollable. Proust's characters wish to understand reality and control it, but reality not only defeats them, it mocks them : the intelligent and refined Charles Swann, try as he might, cannot capture his Odette, when he is in love with her, but after he has lost all interest in her—'*une femme qui ne me plaisait pas, qui n'était pas mon genre*'[5] ('a woman I didn't like, who was not my type')—fate allows him to marry her.

Beckett may or may not share Proust's highly sensitive reactions to experience. In Proust's case there were physiological and psychological reasons for his extreme sensitivity. This would be a biographical question about Beckett, and the biographical material available on Beckett is not very extensive. The idea that reality is intractable and illogical, however, is one that Beckett would agree with wholeheartedly. This view of life has since become the basis of that currently so popular concept, the Absurd. It has a long history.

Proust probably received it in part—especially the idea that life alternates between pain and boredom—from the works of Arthur Schopenhauer, who was very popular among Parisian intellectuals during Proust's younger years. It is interesting to speculate that Proust may be a possible link between Beckett and the most pessimistic of all the nineteenth-century pessimists. Beckett's later characters, with their inexplicable and inescapable need to keep on moving and thinking, look very much like pawns of Schopenhauer's Will.

Probably another reason that Beckett found Proust's thought so congenial is that Proust's idea of the individual as a succession of selves in constant change provided a more complex and therefore more adequate picture of human psychology than could a simple dualism like that of Descartes. Proust, like Beckett, saw human reality as fragmentary. This interpretation of man has several corrollaries. For one thing, an individual made up of a series of sets of habits will very likely be the seat of multiple conflicts, between old and new habits, and between simultaneous conflicting habits. The works of both Proust and Beckett are filled with examples of such inner conflicts. Another corollary is that if an individual is a series of selves, he will never be able to know himself completely in any given moment of time; he would at best be able to know only the self of that particular moment, and even this would be difficult. This is one of the reasons Proust decided to write *A la recherche du temps perdu*, that by writing a fictional re-creation of his life as a whole he might be able to construct a total self, in a way, by making all of his fragmentary selves co-present in memory. Many of Beckett's characters seem to be trying to do the same thing. Moran and Molloy, in *Molloy*, are both writing accounts of their experiences in what seem to be attempts to bring some sort of order into the chaos of their lives; the narrators of the other parts of the trilogy, Malone and the Unnamable, are also compulsive story-tellers, and the stories they tell are either the stories of their own lives or of those of characters who closely resemble them.

The idea that each individual is composed of a temporal series of distinct selves does not have to mean that the successive selves do not involve a certain continuity. In the thought of both Proust and Beckett the personalities that make up the successive stages of one's life tend to be only all too similar. Since they are all subject to the human condition, they all share the same limitations and a tendency to make the same mistakes over and over again. In the case of Beckett, this view of human nature led him to the development of one of his most important themes, that of cyclical time. The idea that time goes through repetitious patterns is implicit in Proust, but in Beckett it is quite elaborately developed. Watt, leaving Knott's house, has learned that there is no certain knowledge of reality, but nothing can prevent his 'for ever falling' into the same 'old error,' the mistake of trying to understand the unintelligible. The Unnamable is the most lucid of Beckett's characters, the most aware that all attempts to explain reality are futile, but his very lucidity only makes him the more frustrated at his inability to stop trying to devise explanations.

This repetitious or cyclical character of human behaviour helps to explain the great family resemblance among Beckett's protagonists. In the novels especially, it almost seems that each protagonist is a sort of reincarnation of the ones who appeared in the preceding novels. The idea of reincarnation in the traditional sense of the word is never explicitly advocated, however. The various narrators can be interpreted either as quite separate and distinct or as a series of personalities within a single abiding person; from Beckett's point of view it would make little difference which interpretation was chosen. Human beings are in states of constant inner flux, but the patterns of flux vary little from person to person. All the patterns are repetitions of the same human compulsions: the compulsion to explain the inexplicable, to impose meaning on the meaningless; the compulsion to be constantly active, in mind, in body, or in both; and the compulsion to try futilely to escape into stasis, mental silence, or nonbeing.

Beckett's first published story, 'Assumption' (1929),[6] does not define the problems of human existence in much detail, but it does describe the desire to escape from them. The nameless protagonist, disgusted with the life force that makes him and others go on thinking, talking, and living, tries to stifle all sound, all his mental processes, thereby damming up into a 'flesh-locked sea of silence' a reservoir of vital energy that he feels threatens to rebel, burst forth, and destroy him. The possibility of his destruction both appeals to him and frightens him. Like so many of Beckett's other characters, he is torn between the desire to die and a persistent, irrational fear of dying.

Then 'the Woman' comes to him. Far from reawakening his
desire to live, she only drives him further from life. Her fatuity
and her 'charming shabbiness' annoy him sufficiently that her
presence diminishes little by little 'the unreasonable tenacity with
which he shrank from dissolution.' As he becomes progressively
more detached from life, he enjoys periods of a certain mental
release, what Murphy would later call the 'Belacqua bliss,' but this
offers no enduring peace because it only lasts for short periods,
after which he has to return to the torment of ordinary consciousness :

> Thus each night he died and was God, each night revived
> and was torn, torn and battered with increasing grievousness,
> so that he hungered to be irretrievably engulfed in the light
> of eternity, one with the birdless cloudless colourless skies, in
> infinite fulfilment.

Permanent release can be found only in death. Finally in a sudden
explosion, 'a great storm of sound, shaking the very house with
its prolonged, triumphant vehemence,' he dies. The woman is left
behind alone, 'caressing his wild dead hair.'

The next important work of fiction Beckett published was *More
Pricks than Kicks* (1934).[7] Actually this work is something between
a novel and a collection of short stories. It was based or another
novel that Beckett abandoned, 'Dream of Fair to Middling Women.'
The 'Dream' was about the same central character, Belacqua Shuah,
and a few sections of it were incorporated in more or less revised
forms into the later volume.[8] Although two of the sections of *More
Pricks than Kicks,* 'Dante and the Lobster' and 'Yellow,' have been
published separately as stories in their own right, the book really
seems more like a novel than like a mere collection of stories
since the stories all focus on the same character and together relate
his life in chronological sequence from his student days to his
burial.

As was mentioned earlier, Beckett's Belacqua, like Dante's, is
'sinfully indolent, bogged in indolence' (p. 44). Like Beckett, too,
perhaps : Peggy Guggenheim called Beckett 'Oblomov' after the
indolent protagonist of Goncharov's novel, and she says that when
she had him read the book he too saw the resemblance between
himself and the Russian writer's inactive hero.[9] If Beckett was

painting a self-portrait in Belacqua, or a portrait of certain aspects of himself, it was not, however, a self-indulgent portrait. The narrator's attitude toward Belacqua is actually, as will appear in the discussion that follows, very critical.

Belacqua is indeed indolent. He claims to be an author, but he has never published anything. He spends most of his life just wandering around avoiding work and any entanglements with other people that would demand much expenditure of energy on his part. He is completely self-centred. In the first story, 'Dante and the Lobster,' his principal preoccupation is his lunch, which can be enjoyed only in complete privacy. Although he thinks occasionally about a murderer named McCabe, who is to be hanged, the pity he likes to think he feels is really very superficial. He spreads out the newspaper with McCabe's face staring up at him, and proceeds to prepare on it his all-important sandwich. 'The crumbs,' says the narrator, 'as though there were no such thing as a sparrow in the wide world, were swept in a fever away' (p. 4). In 'Ding Dong,' while out for a walk, he sees a little girl run down by a car, but is completely indifferent; he just walks right on by.

The type of isolation from humanity that these instances represent is one of the important themes of the book. Belacqua's isolation is due in part to the basic inability, intrinsic in human nature, of any two individuals to adequately communicate their inner lives to one another. This is another idea Beckett shares with Proust. In the second story, 'Fingal,' for example, when Belacqua takes one of his girl friends, Winnie, for a walk, their moods vary, but they never coincide—'Now it was she who was sulky and he who was happy' (p. 26)—and their responses to the countryside, which Belacqua is especially fond of, are completely divergent and drive them further apart : 'He would drop the subject, he would not try to communicate Fingal, he would lock it up in his mind' (p. 27).

Primarily, however, Belacqua's isolation is by preference. The same story, 'Fingal,' ends with Belacqua leaving Winnie with a Dr Sholto, stealing a bicycle—like many of Beckett's later characters, Belacqua loves bicycles—and sneaking off to solitude in a pub : 'Thus they were all met together in Portrane, Winnie, Belacqua, his heart, and Dr Sholto, and paired off to the satisfaction of all parties' (p. 36).

It seems to be mainly out of indolence that Belacqua chooses his isolation. Interpersonal relations, especially where women are

B

involved, can demand rather a lot of energy. Sexual relations, to Belacqua, are more exhausting than pleasurable. When he becomes engaged to another of his girl friends, Lucy, he tries to persuade her to take a lover so that he might be spared the labor of sexual intercourse and be free to devote himself entirely to the less demanding erotic gratifications of what he calls 'private experiences' and 'sursum corda' (p. 150), that is, spying on lovers copulating in the woods. 'Corda is good,' thinks Lucy to herself. Although Lucy rebels at his suggestion that their life together be 'like a music' while she is the wife in body of another, the problem settles itself when she is hit by a car and crippled for life. Forced to be sexless, their marriage is indeed 'like a music' until her death a year or so later.

In spite of his attachment to his solitude, however, Belacqua shows a limited but definite need for fellowship. Although his sorrow at Lucy's death seems characteristically egocentric—'he tended to be sorry for himself when she died' (p. 161)—he also seems to sense that in losing her he lost something more valuable than merely an easy life : the narrator tells us that Belacqua felt keenly 'the lack of those windows on to better worlds that Lucy's big black eyes had been.' And there is also the fact that he marries not just once during the book but three times. He may have married Thelma née bboggs, his next wife, mainly for her father's money, but from the impassioned tone of the love-letter in 'The Smeraldina's Billet-doux,' from 'the Smeraldina,' a German girl who becomes his last wife, it sounds as if there must have been some emotion between them. Even the Smeraldina, of course, finds it difficult to understand Belacqua's disinterest in sex—'why can't he give that what I have been longing for for the last six months?' (p. 221)—and she is shocked by what sounds as if it must be a suggestion on Belacqua's part that she too take a cicisbeo, but there is nothing in the book to suggest that Belacqua marries her for money as he had Thelma. He seems simply to need company. He likes to think of himself as above the need to communicate with others, but in this as in many other matters, he overestimates himself : '. . . his anxiety to explain himself,' says the narrator, '. . . constituted a break-down in the self-sufficiency which he never wearied of arrogating to himself . . .' (p. 45).

Probably the main reason Belacqua needs communication with others is that it can serve as a temporary distraction from a basically burdensome existence. In *Proust*, Beckett spoke of friendship in Proust's thought as one of those mechanisms of habit, 'somewhere between fatigue and ennui' (*Proust*, p. 47), by which a person tries to protect himself from the fundamental pain of life. Many of Beckett's other characters also use social relationships in this way. Molloy, for example, several novels later, out of 'craving for a fellow' (*Molloy*, p. 19), sets out in quest of his mother, though he has no idea what he will say to her or ask from her when he finds her. Malone, in *Malone Dies*, thinks of trapping a little girl for company. In *Waiting for Godot*, Didi and Gogo talk continually of splitting up, but they cannot bring themselves ever to do it. In almost all of Beckett's central characters there is a clearly visible conflict between the 'craving for a fellow' and a craving for solitude.

Another trait Belacqua shares, at least in his younger days, with Beckett's later characters is the need to keep constantly moving from place to place. This is in spite of physical impairments that also link him with other Beckett characters: 'Belacqua had a spavined gait, his feet were in ruins . . .' (p. 10). Belacqua likes to think that it is by choice that he keeps constantly moving. In the later novels, Beckett's characters gradually come to realize that they are forced to keep going by a mysterious inner compulsion. For all of Belcqua's belief in his own freedom, the same compulsion seems to be at work in his case too :

> My sometime friend Belacqua enlivened the last phase of his solipsism, before he toed the line and began to relish the world, with the belief that the best thing he had to do was to move constantly from place to place. He did not know how this conclusion had been gained, but that it was not thanks to his preferring one place to another he felt sure. He was pleased to think he could give what he called the Furies the slip by merely setting himself in motion [p. 43].

In Beckett's world, nobody ever becomes free for long from 'the Furies.' All of his principal characters are driven more or less constantly to keep moving, talking, writing, or thinking. There can be no freedom, no enduring rest. Nor does it matter much where they go or what they do. More often than not they move in circles. If they move in space like Belacqua, they tend to return to the places from which they started: 'The simplest form of this exercise was boomerang, out and back' (*More Pricks*, p. 44). If they are sitting and thinking, as the Unnamable seems to be, they tend to keep repeating patterns of thought that they have already exhausted and repudiated. This is what makes time seem cyclical and inexorable in Beckett's world. Time is the measure of movement, whether physical movement or the movement of thoughts. In the world of Beckett's novels, movement is the basic irresistible reality of life, and this movement tends infernally to repeat the same patterns over and over.

Belacqua does not really understand all this very clearly, but he does have some sense of the constant movement of time and of the boring circularity of its patterns, and at times his sense of this becomes acute and anguished. In the story, 'Ding Dong,' during one of his 'moving pauses,' as he calls his walks, he stops in a pub for a while to 'wait for a sign' before continuing. The sign, when it comes, is not only disappointing but deeply disturbing: an old woman comes along selling 'seats in heaven, tuppence each.' This would sound like a way out of the cycles of time, but the woman goes on to say that 'heaven goes round . . . and round and round and round and round and round' (p. 56). As she whirls her arms to illustrate the idea, her speech accelerates with a dizzying effect: ' "Rowan" she said, dropping the *d*'s and getting more of a spin into the slogan, "rowan an' rowan an' rowan".' Finally Belacqua breaks out into 'a beastly sweat.' There is no escape from time and movement, not even, as Schopenhauer would have believed, in the supposedly timeless heaven of aesthetic contemplation; the spectator in the theater gallery, 'heaven,' is no freer than the actors he watches or the characters they act. As though symbolically capitulating to the inexorable fate the old woman personifies, Belacqua allows her to coerce him into buying four tickets he does not want, 'fer yer friend, yer da, yer ma an' yer motte,' not even one for himself.

In the next story, 'A Wet Night,' Belacqua receives a similar revelation from an advertising sign. It is the Christmas season, and Belacqua is walking along a street on which many displays celebrate Christ's nativity. A Bovril sign shows a series of changing pictures representing the Annunciation. The Annunciation itself, which in the Christian tradition is supposed to represent the manifestation of the purpose of time and a revitalization of the world, here seems empty, tawdry, and tired : 'The lemon of faith jaundiced, annunciating the series, was in a fungus of hopeless green reduced to shingles and abolished' (p. 61). At the end of its hopeless message the sign, like time itself, begins all over again 'da capo.'

Immersed in a meaningless world and driven to the point of exhaustion by irrational needs to keep moving and thinking in spite of his natural indolence, Belacqua naturally thinks at times of escape, especially in his younger years. During the walk in the Fingal countryside with Winnie, he tells her how he would like to be back in the womb, 'in the caul, on my back in the dark for ever' (p. 32). He also seems, like Murphy later, to think of insanity as a possible means of escape : when he and Winnie see the Portrane Lunatic Asylum in the distance, he tells her, 'my heart's right there' (p. 27). In 'Love and Lethe,' he sets out with another girl friend, Ruby Tough, to commit a double suicide. Neither is able to go through with it, though. In the process of getting their paraphernalia ready—veronal, a gun, a suicide note reading 'temporarily sane' on an old automobile licence plate—they end up copulating instead.

Later as he gets older and death becomes a more imminent possibility, Belacqua becomes increasingly reluctant to let go of the life that oppresses him. In its cyclical character, time, eternally repetitious, is overpoweringly boring, and for this reason it drives one to want to escape from consciousness into death, unconsciousness, or madness. But time, in Beckett's works, is not only cyclical, it is also linear. Though a person's life is filled with repeated patterns of frustration and futility, time is always carrying one through steadily increasing physical debility toward death, and as death draws closer, it becomes frightening.

Many of the characters in *More Pricks than Kicks* are disturbed by the passage of time and the approach of death. Ruby Tough is dying of an incurable disease. The Smeraldina has 'some dam thing' on her leg, 'full of matter.' Signorina Ottolenghi, Belacqua's beautiful and elegant Italian teacher in 'Dante and the Lobster,' is past the bloom of her youth, and although she 'had found being young and beautiful and pure more of a bore than anything else' (p. 15), her regret at aging can be seen in the tone of her references to passing time : ' "That used to be" her past tenses were always sorrowful "a favourite question." ' The inevitable decay of life in time presses upon the whole world of this book, as it does in all

of Beckett's works. Balacqua notices on one of his walks the motto
of the college in Pearse Street : '*Perpetuis futuris temporibus dura-
turum*' ('It will last into endless future times'; p. 49). It is 'to be
hoped so indeed,' thinks Belacqua of this quixotic hope for per-
manence. In the world these books present to us, all of life—people,
institutions, everything—is under sentence of decay and death; only
the patterns they live through are permanent.

    Much as Belacqua would like to escape, the fear of death binds
him to life. As we have seen, his one serious attempt to commit
suicide collapses in copulation, which is especially ironic since this
is one of the elements of life that he particularly shuns when he
can. At times he even seizes on pain in order to intensify his sense
of existing. In 'A Wet Night,' he deliberately squeezes a large anthrax that is growing on his neck because the pangs are 'a guarantee
of identity' (p. 95). Years later when he is about to be operated on
for the same anthrax in the story, 'Yellow,' he is terrified that he
may die. The title of the story was probably taken in part from
the color of 'the grand old yaller wall' (p. 242) as the sun shines
on it. The sunlight on the wall looks to Belacqua like a clock
marking the minutes that lead so inexorably toward the operation.
As he watches it and waits, he curses 'this dribble of time,' which
he likens to sanies dripping into a bucket. 'The world wants a new
washer,' he thinks and resolves to draw the blinds. But time cannot
be stopped. Before he can carry out his resolve, a nurse comes in
and prepares him for the operation, during which he is to die of
an overdose of anaesthetic. Some years earlier when he was marrying
his second wife, Thelma, he was given a clock for a wedding
present. It horrified him :

    He who of late years and with the approval of Lucy would
    not tolerate a chronometer of any kind in the house, for whom
    the local publication of the hours was six of the best on the
    brain every hour, and even the sun's shadow a torment, now to
    have this time-fuse deafen the rest of his days [p. 183].

To avoid being constantly reminded by it that the time-fuse would
eventually explode in his death, he decided to turn its 'death's
head' to the wall. But he could no more escape time then by that
means than he can now by drawing the blinds. Both the hands of
the clock going around and around and the sun going around in

the heavens symbolize the inexorable linear movement of time toward decay and death and the inevitable circularity of time's patterns.

One of Belacqua's principal literary interests in this book is Dante, and as could be expected, his attitude toward this figure tells us as much about Belacqua himself as it does about Dante. The story, 'Dante and the Lobster,' has as its organizing principle the conflict between Dante's world view and the reality of the world Belacqua lives in. The story opens :

> It was morning and Belacqua was stuck in the first of the canti in the moon. He was so bogged that he could move neither backward nor forward. Blissful Beatrice was there, Dante also, and she explained the spots on the moon to him [p. 1].

This abrupt opening suggests the completeness of Belacqua's absorption in what he is reading. He is studying Dante in preparation for Signorina Ottolenghi's Italian lesson. His problem is that he can neither understand the argument about the moon-spots, nor abandon it. Like so many of Beckett's other characters, he has a compulsion to think and to understand, even if what he is trying to understand seems hopelessly trivial to him. From Belacqua's point of view, the argument is completely invalid, yet he is intent upon unraveling it in order to understand the nature of the satisfaction it conferred upon 'the misinformed poet.' He would much rather wrestle with what he considers Dante's outdated beliefs than read the writings of nineteenth-century political thinkers like Manzoni or Carducci. He feels no concern with society or with the political systems that try to organize it. For Belacqua, man's real problem is the universe.

The argument to explain the nature of the moon-spots is outdated medieval science, but what is really important is that for Dante, in addition to being a physical phenomenon, they symbolize the mark on the brow of Cain that God put there after the killing of Abel. At issue is the question of the justice of the universe. God, for no apparent reason, preferred the offering of the shepherd, Abel, to that of his brother Cain, the 'tiller of the ground.' This problem of the arbitrariness of the universe, choosing some for good fortune and some for disaster, is a recurrent motif in Beckett's works. One thinks of the two boys who tend Godot's sheep and

goats in *Waiting for Godot*. The shepherd gets beaten, but the
goatherd doesn't. The story of the two thieves crucified with Christ
is another instance of the same theme. It and the story of Abel
and Cain are referred to frequently in Beckett's works. Musing
on the arbitrariness of God's justice, Belacqua imagines what Cain
must have thought: 'It was a mix-up in the mind of the tiller,
but that did not matter. It had been good enough for his mother,
it was good enough for him' (p. 5).

It was good enough for Dante, too, but not for Belacqua. Dante
had accepted on faith the justice of God's judgment, just as he
accepted Beatrice's explanation of the moon-spots—'She had it
from God, therefore he could rely on its being accurate in every
particular' (p. 1)—but Belacqua feels constrained by his own sense
of justice to protest against both God and Dante. Signorina Ottolenghi speaks at one point of 'Dante's rare movements of compassion in Hell' (p. 15). They *are* rare, and even those intermittent
feelings of pity for the damned are opposed by Dante's mentor
Vergil. Belacqua asks Signorina Ottolenghi how she would translate
the pun, '*Qui vive la pietà quando è ben morta*' (*Inferno*, XX 28,
quoted in *More Pricks*, p. 16). The word '*pietà*' means both pity
and piety, so the line means, 'Here lives pity when it should be
dead,' with the extra connotation that may be roughly para-
phrased, 'What kind of piety is this?' These are the words of
Vergil to Dante at the time of one of his rare movements of compassion. 'Why not piety and pity both, even down below,' thinks
Belacqua, 'Why not mercy and godliness together?' (p. 17). But
he goes on to think with disgust that there is no mercy either in
Dante's world or his own : 'He thought of Jonah and the gourd and
the pity of a jealous God on Nineveh. And poor McCabe, he would
get it in the neck at dawn.'

The story's criticism of Dante is, however, double-edged. Belacqua's compassion for suffering humanity is really no deeper than
Dante's. He thinks indignantly of how McCabe, the murderer,
will hang, but the thought of the hanging spices his lunch (p. 13).
Another symbol of suffering is the lobster that Belacqua is going
to eat for dinner. When he picks up the lobster at the fishmonger's,
he does not realize that it is still living and that his aunt will have
to boil it alive before they will be able to eat it. Later he is
horrified when he and his aunt open the package to find the live
lobster shuddering, 'exposed cruciform' on the kitchen table.

Belacqua's aunt, however, points out his moral inconsistency : 'You make a fuss . . . and upset me and then lash into it for your dinner' (p. 20). Unwilling to give up his dinner, Belacqua tries to persuade himself that the lobster will not suffer much : 'Well, thought Belacqua, it's a quick death, God help us all.' The narrator comments, 'It is not.' Belacqua is really no more willing than Dante to risk the consequences of defying the universe.

In this instance, as in many others, Belacqua is something of a poseur. He claims to be a man of compassion, but compassion must not prevent his enjoying his dinner. He claims to be an author without ever having actually published anything. He constantly employs French phrases to display his learning and alludes frequently to his not really very extensive Continental travels : 'You make great play with your short stay abroad,' thinks Winnie as he compares the Fingal countryside to Saône et Loire.

Belacqua's most pretentious pose is that of self-sufficiency. He likes to think of himself as capable of living, as Murphy would later want to, free from worldly attachments in the Cartesian heaven of his mind. 'He was an indolent bourgeois poltroon,' says the narrator, 'very talented up to a point, but not fitted for private life in the best and brightest sense, in the sense to which he referred when he bragged of how he furnished his mind and lived here, because it was the last ditch when all was said and done' (p. 233).

The narrator does not tell us what Belacqua's talents are, but his greatest talent seems to be for self-deception. When his pity for the lobster would interfere with his dinner, he can persuade himself that it will not really suffer. When he fails to commit suicide in 'Love and Lethe' and ends up copulating instead, the narrator speculates : 'It will quite possibly be his boast in years to come, when Ruby is dead and he an old optimist, that at least on this occasion, if never before nor since, he achieved what he set out to do . . .' (p. 138).

The narrator's attitude toward Belacqua is critical throughout. He says explicitly that Belacqua was 'an impossible person' (p. 46) and that he gave him up finally 'because he was not serious.' What the narrator probably means by 'not serious' is that whereas a person might have many delusions both about himself and about life and yet be honestly mistaken, Belacqua was not honest even with himself. His poses were a substitute for serious wrestling with the real problems of life. All of Beckett's characters suffer a variety of delusions, but most of them try at least some of the time to see the problems—pain, boredom, compulsions to keep moving and think-ing—as clearly as they can and to deal with them directly. Beckett treats all his characters ironically, but Belacqua is the only one who is treated caustically.

Actually, in none of Beckett's subsequent works is the critical attitude toward the protagonist so strongly pronounced. In *More Pricks than Kicks*, the narrator calls Belacqua 'impossible.' In *Murphy*, the narrator, although he is quite critical of his central character, also has a certain respect for him. In *Watt*, the narrator, at least in part of the work, seems to be a fellow inmate of Watt's in an asylum. Watt is simply an interesting puzzle to him, not an object of moral judgment. In the remaining novels, the trilogy and *How It Is*, the characters narrate their own stories in the first person; the irony is still there, but the reader is left to detect it for himself from their inconsistencies, evasions, and omissions.

CHAPTER III

Murphy

> The sun shone, having no alternative on the nothing new.
> Murphy sat out of it, as though he were free, in a mew in West
> Brompton.

The opening of *Murphy*[1] is a marvel of compression. The lines
above, and the next few pages that follow them, summarize with
great compactness and precision the basic situation of the book.
As in *More Pricks than Kicks*, the sun is the symbol of time's inexorableness and its cyclical, repetitious character. The sun has no
alternative; time moves on, and the processes of decay move with
it. The mew in which Murphy sits 'out of it, as though he were
free' has been condemned, and soon he will have to rouse himself
and find new quarters. But for all of this linear, forward movement
of time, the sun repeats its journey through the heavens in the
same cyclical pattern every day and every year: 'The poor old
sun' is 'in the Virgin again for the billionth time' (pp. 1-2). Although
'the light never waned the same way twice' (p. 7), nothing is ever
new.

Murphy is sitting in his rocking chair in a corner curtained
off from the sun trying to withdraw from this world into the freedom of his mind. To do this is not easy, and as the book progresses, it becomes clear that all freedom, even that which Murphy
thinks he finds or could ultimately find in the mind, is illusory.
As though to assert its power and to mock its victim, the world
breaks into Murphy's revery for a moment before letting him go on:
'Somewhere a cuckoo-clock, having struck between twenty and

thirty, became the echo of a street-cry, which now entering the mew
gave *Quid pro quo*! *Quid pro quo*! directly' (p. 2). The chiming of
the hours symbolically mingles with the cry of the street-seller,
a member of those business circles that cultivate 'the sense of time as
money' (p. 70). This is a world that Murphy, during most of his life,
has had as little to do with as possible : 'These were sights and
sounds that he did not like. They detained him in the world to
which they belonged, but not he, as he fondly hoped' (p. 2). The
word 'fondly,' of course, means 'dearly,' but it also has the implication, 'foolishly,' as the book later makes clear.

Pursuing his fond hope, Murphy is trying to 'come alive in his
mind.' What this means is fully described in Chapter VI of the
book. Murphy's picture of the relationship between body and mind
is Cartesian or, to be more precise, occasionalist : as was mentioned
before, he has even read Geulincx (see p. 178). His mind pictures
itself 'as a large hollow sphere, hermetically closed to the universe
without' (p. 107). This does not involve Murphy 'in the idealist tar'
(p. 108) of a thinker such as Berkeley, however. He does not believe
that the mind is the only reality; mind and body are both 'equally
real if not equally pleasant.' He does not understand how the two
can be connected, but he takes it for granted that they are. As
far as Murphy is concerned, the nature of the connection is not
important; what is important is that he be able to forget the
body from time to time in order to enjoy life in the mind : '. . .
life in his mind gave him pleasure, such pleasure that pleasure was
not the word' (p. 2).

Murphy's mind appears to him to be divided into three zones,
'light, half light, dark, each with its specialty' (p. 111). The 'light'
is the zone of simple imagination. In it, Murphy can enjoy imagining the world to be a pleasanter place than it is : 'Here the kick that
the physical Murphy received, the mental Murphy gave. . . . Here
the whole physical fiasco became a howling success.' More removed
from the world, and therefore pleasanter than this, is the 'half light.'
This is a realm of detached contemplation, where he can experience
what he calls 'the Belacqua bliss.' Murphy has an elaborate, but
rather distorted, fantasy of the antepurgatory in which he imagines
Dante's Belacqua to have been in such bliss. Actually, Dante's
Belacqua had hoped that an '*orazione . . . che surga su di cuor che
in grazia viva*'[2] ('a prayer . . . arising from the heart of one who
lives in grace,' *Purgatorio*, IV. 133-34) might free him from part

of the time he was required to wait in the antepurgatory before proceeding through purgation to the real bliss in paradise. Murphy, however, who genuinely seems to believe that he will find himself in the antepurgatory after death, hopes that he will live to be quite old so that he may spend a long time sitting there 'in the lee of Belacqua's rock' enjoying his 'embryonal repose' (pp. 77-78). Even this bliss, though, is not the total escape he would ideally like. He would like to be free even from the exercise of freedom: '. . . the choice of bliss introduced an element of effort . . .' (p. 113). His ideal is the 'dark,' a kind of mental chaos, 'nothing but commotion and the pure forms of commotion' (p. 112). In this mental region prior to rationality and individuality, he would be 'not free, but a mote in the dark of absolute freedom.'

Murphy's ultimate goal, then, is a refinement on the ante-purgatory. He does not want merely to be Belacqua sitting in the lee of a rock; he wants to become the rock itself. What he wants is a condition of absolute absence of will, a condition even beyond indolence. That this goal is unattainable is made clear by the remainder of the book. At the very least he will have to leave his chair to find a new refuge since the mew has been condemned. Besides, there is his attachment to Celia.

Some six months before, Murphy had left Ireland, the land of his birth, to come to the mew in London. He had been studying with a man named Neary to learn how to modify the extremes of his extremely irregular heart. Having failed to learn this Apmonia, Isonomy, or Attunement, as Neary called it, Murphy decided to leave the country, probably to escape his 'tired' and 'depraved' (p. 6) entanglement with a Miss Counihan. A few months later, he met Celia, a beautiful, young Irish prostitute, while she was walking her beat in West Brompton. The world is tenacious; no sooner did Murphy disentangle himself from one woman than he became involved with another.

If *Murphy* is to some extent a parody of Dante's *Purgatorio*, then Celia is the Beatrice of the book. Dante's Beatrice, through her agent, Vergil, guided Dante out of the antepurgatory and up the mountain of purgation so that finally, in the *Paradiso*, she could lead him herself into the direct vision of *'l'amor che move il sole e l'altre stelle'* ('the love that moves the sun and the other stars,' *Paradiso*, XXXIII. 145). Celia would like to lead Murphy out of his own 'Belacqua bliss' into a life of love. The difference is that

whereas Beatrice, whose name means 'she who makes blessed,' was
guiding Dante to a state of blessedness outside time, Murphy's
Celia, whose name ('heavenly') suggests her relationship to the solar
and sidereal cycles of the temporal system, is trying to draw
Murphy into an acceptance of time as the concomitant and price
of love.

Celia is treated very sympathetically in this book. In fact, she
is the only really beautiful and appealing female character Beckett
has ever created. She is warm and generous, and she genuinely
loves Murphy. Although Murphy resists his attraction to her as
best he can—'The part of him that he hated [his body] craved
for Celia, the part that he loved [his mind] shrivelled up at the
thought of her' (p. 8)—the fact that he finds this attraction so strong
makes him seem more human than the Belacqua of *More Pricks
than Kicks*, who was totally, almost subhumanly, egocentric. As it
turns out, Celia's very love for him eventually enables her to
understand Murphy's view of life and to let him go. She even takes
to sitting in his rocking chair and dreaming. It is as if Dante's
Belacqua were to persuade both Dante and Beatrice to come and
dawdle with him through all eternity in the antepurgatory.

At the time that the book opens, though, Celia is still trying
to persuade Murphy to join the world. She has been making her
own living as a prostitute, but now she wants him to make a living
for them both. Murphy does not see why she should not go on
with her work, but Celia is adamant, and his need for her has made
him accept her conditions. He has sent her out to get a horoscope
to guide him in his search for a job. Now, just as he is beginning
to rock himself into bliss, the phone rings, bringing him symbolically
back to the reality in which he will have to commit himself to the
world of everyday labor. Celia is phoning to tell him that she
is on her way with the horoscope, symbol of the universe of time,
from Ramaswami Krishnaswami Narayanaswami Suk, a swami,
'who cast excellent nativities for sixpence.'

In the weeks that follow, Murphy and Celia move into another
flat and begin what Celia calls their 'new life' (p. 64)—a pun on
La Vita Nuova? Their life together during this time has a genuinely
idyllic quality. When Murphy gets home at night, Celia helps him
out of his suit, feeds him, and 'then, till it was time to push him
out in the morning, serenade, nocturne and albada' (p. 74). In
this respect, Murphy's life differs markedly from that of Belacqua

in *More Pricks than Kicks*. Belacqua not only did not enjoy sex, he considered it a laborious nuisance. Murphy, in contrast, usually arrives home 'impatient for the music to begin' (p. 106), and by 'music' he means something quite different from what Belacqua meant by the same word.

Nevertheless, when Murphy finally does get a job, with a mental asylum named the Magdalen Mental Mercyseat, he becomes so fascinated by the idea of association with the insane that he loses all interest in Celia. After he gets his rocker and a gas stove installed in his garret at the Mercyseat, he never returns to her. In the asylum he, for the first time, finds people who appear to him to represent the ideal life he has so long been seeking. His special hero is a Mr Endon, whose name means 'within' in Greek,[3] a schizoid who seems to be totally oblivious to the world of outer reality. He appears to Murphy to be the living embodiment of the 'dark,' that region of the mind in which absolute freedom consists in the absence of freedom. At times Murphy feels that there is hope that he himself might one day attain the perfection of psychosis. When Ticklepenny, the homosexual male nurse who helped Murphy get the position in the asylum because he was himself afraid of going mad if he continued in it, tells Murphy one day that he is beginning to resemble the lunatics, Murphy's 'gratified look' (p. 193) is unnerving to him. At other times, however, Mr Endon and the other 'higher schizoids' seem to Murphy to be unapproachably beyond him.

This is Murphy's state of mind during his first night on night-duty, his last night on earth. As he begins his second round of the cells 'with a heavy heart' (p. 240), Murphy sees that Mr Endon has set up a chess set in his cell. During the intermissions between rounds, he plays chess with Mr Endon—a strange game in which Mr Endon's sole activity is completely to avoid contact with his opponent—and finally falls asleep over the board in a vision of formlessness. Mr Endon escapes and wreaks havoc in the ward. When Murphy wakes up and goes to find him, Mr Endon is turning on and off the light in a hypomanic's cell: 'The hypomanic bounced off the walls like a bluebottle in a jar' (p. 247). Murphy puts Mr Endon to bed, leaves the ward, and returns to his garret. Later that night, the gas stove in the garret explodes and blows Murphy to pieces.

It is never made clear in the book, either to the other characters on to the reader, whether Murphy's death is suicide or merely an accident. On the one hand, as Murphy is putting Mr Endon to bed, he hears inside himself and speaks out loud the words, 'The last Mr Murphy saw of Mr Endon was Mr Murphy unseen by Mr Endon. This was also the last Murphy saw of Murphy' (p. 250). These words express Murphy's despair of ever being completely able to share Mr Endon's isolation, and they seem to predict Murphy's suicide. There is also the fact that Murphy leaves behind a note addressed to 'Mrs Murphy,' with directions for disposing of his remains. On the other hand, however, when Murphy returns to his garret and settles down in his rocking chair, he dimly intends, as the narrator tells us, 'to have a short rock and then, if he felt any better, to dress and go . . . back to Brewery Road, to Celia, serenade, nocturne, albada' (p. 252). As he begins to feel better, drifting away into his mind, the gas goes on : 'The gas went on in the w.c., excellent gas, superfine chaos' (p. 253). Murphy could not possibly turn it on himself from his garret. It is piped in from a connection in the W.C., where the chain that turns it on is easily mistaken for the toilet chain. The gas chain has even been pulled by accident before (see p. 174). Did Murphy choose to sit there with a candle on the floor in order to leave it to chance to see if he would be blown up? We are given no explanation, and perhaps this is as it should be. The world of this book is one in which all sorts of puzzling events simply have to be accepted. For example, a character named Cooper, who has not been able to take his hat off or sit down in many years, suddenly finds himself after Murphy's death able to do both. He does not know why this sudden change takes place, 'nor did he pause to inquire' (p. 273). In a universe as unpredictable as this, perhaps it would be quixotic to look for explanations. At any rate, Murphy's story had to end with his death. His quest for freedom through psychosis had proved futile, and the apparent humanism and life-affirming quality of a return to 'serenade, nocturne, albada' with Celia would not have harmonized at all with the views developed in the rest of the book. Celia herself, by this time, had already become almost as disaffected with life as Murphy.

To return to the story, however, during the time he is working in the asylum, Murphy is being sought for high and low by a number of other characters. Neary and Miss Counihan are probably the most important of these. Another is a person named Wylie, whose personality fits his name. About the time that Murphy begins his job at the Magdalen Mental Mercyseat, these three set out from Dublin to find him. They are accompanied by Cooper, whom they have employed as a detective. Each of them is looking for Murphy for a different purpose. Miss Counihan, for some strange reason, thinks that Murphy has gone to London to make a fortune so that he will be able to marry her and support her in style. Neary, who previously wanted to find Murphy in order to convince Miss Counihan that he himself would be a better choice for her, has by this time lost interest in her and is simply seeking Murphy as a friend with whom he hopes, with a hope that seems as strangely founded as Miss Counihan's, to be able to communicate. Wylie is going along because he hopes to either win Miss Counihan for himself or get money from Neary's second wife for information about Neary's whereabouts. Cooper is accompanying them because he is being employed openly by Neary as a detective to find Murphy, and secretly by all three as a spy against each of the others. As though to illustrate the isolation that separates each human being from every other, the motives of each of these characters change continually, but never coincide. All that they have in common is that for various fluctuating and preposterous reasons they are all seeking Murphy.

All are people immersed in the temporal world, bound to it by a multiplicity of attachments. Murphy, in contrast, has become disillusioned with the world and has severed most of his attachments to it. It is really Murphy's detachment from the world that seems to fascinate the characters seeking him. It is probably this that makes Neary feel that Murphy could be a friend to him; he knows quite well that the others are only interested in him because he has a little more money than they. Even Miss Counihan seems to feel Murphy's attitude toward life is what makes him attractive. She says that the reason she wants Murphy is that he alone is not 'defiled' by 'the crass and unharmonious unison, the mind at the cart-tail of the body, the body at the chariot-wheels of the mind' (p. 218). It is said at one point that what attracts women to Murphy is his 'surgical quality' (p. 62), by which it is apparently meant that he has an air of detached impersonality. Those who are slaves to attachment can hardly help but be impressed by those who are relatively free from it.

Celia, by the time this group meets her, is practically as dis-

illusioned with the world as Murphy is. During the period in which
Murphy and she were enjoying the 'new life' together, she gradually came to see life through Murphy's eyes. As Murphy spent
his days in the streets, halfheartedly job hunting, Celia spent hers
in Murphy's rocker, and in it she came to see the absurdity of the
commercial world that Murphy found so repugnant: 'Thus in
spite of herself she began to understand as soon as he gave up trying
to explain' (p. 67). In the detachment and sympathy arising from
this vision, she found herself able to love him not for what she
would have him become but for what he was. By the time he left
her for the Mercyseat, Celia was able to let him go. Her love for
him had become a generous, sympathetic love that wished him
to be free. When Neary, Counihan, and Wylie eventually come to
her asking for information about Murphy, she tells them that he
is gone because he *had* to leave her, and she expresses the hope
that he has at last found his freedom: 'I was the last exile. . . .
The last, if we are lucky' (p. 234). The narrator adds, 'So love is
wont to end, in protasis, if it be love.' Neary and Wylie seem to
sense the nobility of this detached love in her when they first meet
her. Miss Counihan is blinded by her own feminine envy, but
Neary and Wylie feel 'their lees of finer feeling' cast 'into a sudden
swirl' (p. 231) by the first sight of her. They both stagger 'reverently'
to their feet and, throughout the succeeding interview, gradually
come to feel 'more and more swine before a pearl.'

The whole group settles down to wait for Murphy's return.
Finally, word of his demise comes from the Mercyseat, and they
go there to identify his remains, which is not an easy task after
the explosion. Miss Counihan resents the fact that Celia alone is
able to identify them, on the basis of a large pink naevus on one
of the buttocks—this was prepared for very early in the novel
when Celia, on page 29, was held spellbound by this feature of
Murphy's anatomy. In the note left for 'Mrs Murphy,' Murphy
expressed the wish that his body be cremated and the ashes be
flushed down a toilet in the men's room of the Abbey Theatre,
Dublin. As though to illustrate the resistance of the world to men's
wishes, Murphy's ashes instead are dropped by Cooper on the floor
of a saloon, kicked around and scattered all over the room, and
finally, 'before another dayspring greyened the earth . . . swept
away with the sand, the beer, the butts, the glass, the matches, the
spits, the vomit' (p. 275).

The ending of the book shows Celia returning to a life of loneliness. The last scene finds her helping her aged grandfather, Mr Willoughby Kelly, to sail his kite in a park. As Mr Kelly lets the kite out all the way in order to 'measure the distance from the unseen to the seen' (p. 280), the kite, another symbol of the intractability of the world, escapes, and as he staggers after it, he falls and seriously injures himself. Celia picks his limp body up and wheels him home. He was all she had before Murphy, and if he is now dying, as seems apparent, she will be left totally alone. It is an extremely poignant ending. The loneliness Celia is left to is not only that of a person deprived of those who were close to her; it is that of a person who has come to see clearly the emptiness and hopelessness of life in this world.

Although Celia is the main object of the reader's sympathy in the book, the book is really Murphy's story. It is in Murphy's desire to escape from the conditions of life in the temporal world and in the inadequacies of his efforts to escape that the principal message of the book is to be found.

Like the Belacqua of *More Pricks than Kicks*, Murphy is a rather indolent person—he is said once to have wanted an 'artificial respiration machine to get into when he was fed up breathing' (p. 49)—but his indolence is more complicated than Belacqua's. His desire is not just to avoid effort, but to find a kind of supratemporal salvation. When Celia brought Murphy the horoscope and saw how disturbed he was by the prospect of work, it struck her 'that a merely indolent man would not be so affected by the prospect of employment' (p. 31). Belacqua was indolent in the simplest way, but Murphy is something of a mystic.

Murphy is much more of a thinker than Belacqua, and one of the things he wants to escape from is the need to think. In his younger years he had even been a theological student and had lain awake nights pondering theological problems. At the time the events in the book take place, Murphy is still trying to understand his world and to impose explanations on it. His occasionalist division of himself into body and mind is an example. This is really only a theory that Murphy imposes on a reality that is much less simple. The narrator is careful to dissociate himself from Murphy's way of thinking about his mind : 'Happily we need not concern ourselves with this apparatus as it really was—that would be an extravagance and an impertinence—but solely with what it felt and pictured itself to be' (p. 107). Another example is Murphy's belief in astrology. Astrology, 'the only system outside his own in which he felt the least confidence' (pp. 22-23), is practically a religion to him, though as his solipsism increases later in the book he comes to feel that the stars depend on him rather than he on them. Sometimes his mind even feels a need to think quite apart from any effort to explain things, as when he sits in a park calculating all the possible permutations of the sequences in which he could eat five biscuits. This foreshadows the episode of the sucking stones in *Molloy*.

Murphy is also driven by a compulsion to keep active. He would like to withdraw into the purely passive condition of mental contemplation, but like Belacqua in *More Pricks than Kicks*, who had to keep moving to escape 'the Furies,' Murphy is also driven by Furies to keep active in the world. The principal Fury in Murphy's life during the period described in the book is, of course, his attachment to Celia. When Celia brings him the horoscope that will show him how to find work, she is afraid that he may think of her as 'a Fury coming to carry him off' (p. 27), though she realizes that 'it was not she, but Love, that was the bailiff.'

Belacqua's Furies were vague in nature, like the compulsions that drive the characters of the trilogy later. In *Murphy*, however, almost as if the book had been written from a Hindu or Buddhist point of view, it is attachment that imprisons one in the temporal world and binds one to constant activity. Neary is the most prominent example in the book of a person enslaved by attachments. Neary no sooner ceases to desire one thing or person than he begins to desire another: '. . . he scratches himself out of one itch into the next . . .' (p. 202). In his more lucid moments, Neary wonders if there is not some one desire that once satisfied would not engender new desires: 'Is there no flea that found at last dies without issue? No keyflea?' (p. 201). The narrator says that it was from just this consideration that Murphy had long ago set out to capture himself. As long as one thinks there is anything anywhere that could satisfy desire, one is 'doomed to hope unending,' which condemns one to a life of repetitious patterns of disappointment, 'the old endless chain of love, tolerance, indifference, aversion and disgust' (p. 255).

The oppressive circularity of this kind of life in the temporal world is symbolized by the book's frequent astrological references.

The sun and planets move year after year through the same basic patterns, and the temporal details of the book, as though to emphasize the subjection of all human activity to all-encompassing cyclical patterns, are always described with reference to their positions :

> Celia's triumph over Murphy . . . was gained about the middle of September, Thursday the 12th to be pedantic, a little before the Ember Days, the sun being still in the Virgin. Wylie rescued Neary . . . a week later, as the sun with a sigh of relief passed over into the Balance. The encounter . . . between Murphy and Ticklepenny, took place on Friday, October the 11th . . . the moon being full again. . . .
>
> Let us now take Time that old fornicator, bald though he be behind, by such few sad short hairs as he has, back to Monday, October the 7th, the first day of his restitution to the bewitching Miss Greenwich [p. 114].

The elaborate detailing of temporal sequences in *Murphy* is more than a mere tour-de-force of technique; it symbolizes the nature and the power of time in the universe from which Murphy is trying to escape. Time is an 'old fornicator,' constantly growing older and more decrepit and endlessly repeating his tired encounters. This is a universe in which 'all things limp together for the only possible' (p. 235).

Murphy's goal throughout the book is that of 'checking the starry concave' (p. 21), of freeing himself from the cycles of time. Only his methods of pursuing this goal change. At the beginning, he still hopes to be able to withdraw from time into the pleasanter zones of his mind, but as the book goes on, he comes to realize that although this withdrawal offers temporary relief, he will always be called back from it by Celia or something else. His last desperate hope for permanent release comes to him through the job at the Magdalen Mental Mercyseat. Here in the 'higher schizoids' he finally discovers exemplars of what seems to him to be a state of mind in which one is totally disconnected from the world of time, labor, and desire. The lunatics are actually not at all in the bliss he imagines them to be in, but in his desire for escape he persuades himself that they are.

In reality, Murphy's striving, based though it is on a genuine appreciation of the irksomeness of life in time, is as futile and perhaps even as infantile as the desire, to which it is explicitly compared, of returning to the womb. Murphy never wears a hat because 'the memories it awoke of the caul were too poignant, especially when he had to take it off' (p. 73), and the 'Belacqua bliss' he aspires to after death is supposed to consist in an 'embryonal repose' (p. 78). When he arrives finally at the Mercyseat, he finds there the womblike garret for which he has been seeking high and low, and this is to him only a foretaste of the felicity he hopes to enjoy in the even more womblike padded cells, which are kept always at body temperature and which admit scarcely any contact with the outer world :

> The pads surpassed by far all he had even been able to imagine in the way of indoor bowers of bliss. The three dimensions, slightly concave . . . the pneumatic upholstery, cushioning every square inch of ceiling, walls, floor and door. . . . The temperature was such that only total nudity could do it justice. . . . The compartment was windowless, like a monad, except for the shuttered judas in the door, at which a sane eye appeared . . . at frequent and regular intervals . . . [p. 181].

Murphy's first impression of the life of the insane is that it is exactly what he has always been looking for. It is not this at all, but he wants so much for it to be what he hopes it is that he suppresses any awareness that it is not : 'Nothing remained but to substantiate these [first impressions], distorting all that threatened to belie them. It was strenuous work, but very pleasant' (p. 176). All Murphy's excited joy in his work at the Mercyseat is founded on an illusion perpetuated by self-deception.

The narrator's attitude toward Murphy becomes quite explicitly ironic in this section of the book. Although Murphy is presented as a more intelligent and serious person than was the Belacqua of *More Pricks than Kicks*—'All the puppets in this book whinge sooner or later, except Murphy, who is not a puppet' (p. 122)—Murphy, too, is the object of satire. Honest and clear-sighted in his revulsion toward the temporal world, he makes himself a fool in his attempt to believe that there can be an escape from it. Ignoring or distorting the obvious significance of 'the frequent expressions apparently of pain, rage, despair and in fact all the usual, to which some patients gave vent, suggesting a fly somewhere in the ointment of Microcosmos' (p. 179), Murphy manages to make himself believe that they are 'one and all' enjoying a 'glorious time' (p. 180). The narrator speaks of the whole matter as 'lovingly simplified and perverted by Murphy' (p. 178). In order to explain away the evidence of pain in the lives of the patients, Murphy convinces himself that what pain they experience is caused by the annoying efforts of the physicians to restore them to the 'collossal fiasco' of reality, that the perfect bliss of their cells is broken only by the intruding eye at the judas. By means of these camouflaging explanations, Murphy protects his illusions in order that, 'stimulated by all those lives immured in mind, as he insisted on supposing,' he might labor 'at his own little dungeon in Spain' (p. 180).

Murphy never realizes the truth. He gives up hope finally that he will ever be able to construct and inhabit the castle in Spain of a psychosis, but he never has any idea that even if he could he would find it a dungeon. As he makes his rounds on the last night before he dies, he is 'walking round and round at the foot of the cross' (p. 236) without even realizing that at the centre of his devout orbit is the agony of a crucifixion.

Beckett's books are always satiric because it is of the very essence of the human condition, as they present it, that man is inevitably subject to illusions. A person may divest himself of some illusions, as Murphy has freed himself from many, but he will subsequently cooperate in his subjection to other illusions. Murphy tries much more seriously to see life clearly than Belacqua did, and Watt and the characters of the trilogy will try even harder, but no one can ever be free from the conditions of human life, and in Beckett's world, one of these conditions is illusion. Just as man can never be free from time and the repetitious patterns time leads him through, he can never be free from the necessity to think about his condition and to try to explain it, even if this means imposing an explanation on a reality totally resistant to understanding. Murphy was on guard against the deceptions the external world might try to impose on him, but not sufficiently on guard against the tendency to self-deception that his own desires for clarity and freedom could lead him into.

CHAPTER IV

Watt and the Transition to the Trilogy

Watt, which was written in the early 1940's, though not published until 1953, was a new departure for Beckett. Thematically it is in direct continuity with the earlier works; it simply carries further Beckett's exploration of the human condition, of the repetitiousness of human behaviour, of man's need to keep pursuing useless goals and to keep trying to explain an unintelligible universe. In technique, however, it departs from the realism of the earlier works in order to experiment with a more abstract and archetypal nonrealism. Belacqua and Murphy were odd, but they were odd in a credible way, and the world they lived in would seem recognizably realistic to any reader. In *Watt* and in the novels that follow it, the world will often seem quite normal for a time until suddenly something appears that is obviously pure fantasy. *Watt* opens and closes with groups of ordinary people in a realistic setting, a park at the beginning, a railroad station at the end, but the main body of the work, which the realistic settings enclose like a frame, is a description of a strange household presided over by a fantastic figure, Mr Knott, who continually changes his shape and his entire physical appearance.

The story of *Watt* is extremely simple in outline. It is an archetypal quest in which a person sets out to explore the unknown, encounters it, and then returns to the ordinary world. Like the hero of a traditional quest, Watt represents man as such with the characteristics and failings of human nature. This does not mean that Watt is a typical person, of course. The typical person would be very unlikely to set out on such a quest. Ordinary people, such as the complacent Irish Catholics in the groups at the beginning and at the end, tend to herd together and to cling to the comforts provided by social and religious traditions. They use their illusory certainties to protect themselves from ever having to face the disturbing mysteries that the hero sets out to explore. The reason Watt represents man as such is that he more fully actualizes the potentialities of human nature than do these others. Watt questions the universe in a way they would never be willing to; he faces and responds to a reality they hide from. His questioning, and even his defeat, tell us much about man.

As befits his archetypal role, the characterization of Watt is much more general in outline, less individualized, than were those of Belacqua or Murphy. These characters each had a life history and a personality shaped by particular experiences, their student years, their encounters with women, their disappointments with life. Watt is particularized by physical details, but both his past and his personality are of the vaguest sort. He is a shabby middle-aged man with a big red nose and protruding ears. He has an eccentric way of walking by flinging his legs, held stiff, in directions perpendicular to that toward which he wants to move. He wears a block hat, inherited from his grandfather, and a baggy, thread-bare coat, inherited from his father. One of his shoes is too large, the other too small. He drinks nothing but milk, and he habitually picks his nose. Apart from these details, we are told scarcely anything about him. He is said to have been in London at one time, but there is no account of what he was doing there.[1] Goff Nixon, one of the realistic characters at the opening, who claims to have known Watt for years, can say nothing about him except that he is 'an experienced traveller,' that he has no fixed address, and that he is truthful, mild, and inoffensive.

It is significant that Nixon feels, even though he is much older than Watt, that there was never a time when he did not know him. The reason for this is probably that Watt represents to him a certain aspect of human nature. 'All men by nature desire to know,'[2] said Aristotle. Watt is a living embodiment of this characteristic of man. As his name suggests, Watt is a walking 'What?'

The story of Watt's journey to Knott's house is the story of man's quest for some kind of absolute knowledge that will bring him peace. Man has always sought something of this sort, and many individuals have thought that they have found it. Dante's God was

conceived of as absolute and immutable, and knowledge of Him
was thought to bring complete certainty, peace, and bliss to the
soul that knew Him in the beatific vision. Dante's *Commedia*
describes the soul's ascent to this vision. *Watt* describes a similar
quest of the absolute, but the goal of this quest is exactly opposite
to that of Dante. Knott is no Absolute, and the knowledge gained
from experience of him is the knowledge that no certainty is
possible. The end of Watt's quest is disillusionment.

Watt's disillusionment with the hope of certain knowledge does
not set him free, however, from the need to go on trying to know.
The compulsion to think and to impose meaning on the meaningless is intrinsic to human nature; no man can ever become free
from the vain quest for certainty. But the disillusioned state he
arrives at by the end of the book does distinguish him from the
ordinary people in the railroad station who still believe in the
traditional and, from the point of view of this book, completely
illusory conception of an orderly universe directed benevolently
by the Christian God. Watt's disillusionment is, as Erskine, his
predecessor in Knott's service, predicted it would be, 'quite useless
wisdom . . . dearly won' (p. 62), but it *is* wisdom of a sort. It is
adequate to the reality of his world.

The ordinary people, both at the beginning and at the end,
are intrigued by Watt, but they are also disdainful of him. He is
obviously not a regular member of normal society who participates
in its traditions and shares its confidence in illusory certainties.
The description Nixon gives of Watt at the beginning is that of
a tramp, a person who lives outside the fringe of the social
community. Mrs Nixon suggests that he may be a university man,
which to the ordinary person, the kind of person Mrs Nixon is,
means a man who probably thinks too much for his own good.
When Mr Nixon says Watt is setting out on a journey, Hackett
suggests that it 'might be the best thing for him' if he did not go.
To those who cling to the comforts of society and its traditions,
a person leaving these behind will always appear foolish. These
are people who speak comfortably of the traditional God as though
He were a combination mascot and presiding magistrate. Their
speech is sprinkled with phrases like 'as God is my witness' or
'God forgive.' These are simply conventional phrases, not taken
very seriously, nor is the God they refer to a very vivid reality
to the speakers. When Hackett calls God to witness, the policeman

retorts that 'God is a witness that cannot be sworn' (p. 9). God's place, for these people, is in His heaven, where He serves merely as a comfortable excuse to evade having to face the real absurdity of the universe.

The triviality of the conventional idea of God is further clarified in the episode in which Watt is riding on the train on his way to Knott's house. He shares the compartment with a Mr Spiro—'my friends call me Dum' (p. 27)—editor of *Crux*, a popular Catholic monthly, which keeps its 'tonsure above water' by offering prizes to those who can solve puzzles 'of a devout twist,' such as rearranging the fifteen letters of the Holy Family to form a question and answer. ('Winning entry: *Has J. Jurms a po? Yes.*') The mere fact that such trivia could be thought compatible with the title, *Crux* (*The Cross*), reveals the shallowness of popular Christianity. Spiro is puzzling over some theological questions sent in by one of the magazine's readers:

Sir
A rat, or other small animal, eats of a consecrated wafer.
1)   Does he ingest the Real Body, or does he not?
2)   If he does not, what has become of it?
3)   If he does, what is to be done with him?

The questions trivialize the Christian God by reducing Him from a mystery to a conundrum, but Spiro takes them quite seriously, replying at great length to questions one and three with quotations from Saint Bonaventura, Peter Lombard, Alexander of Hales, Sanchez, Suarez, and others. The whole of theology becomes a mere game. Watt, however, hears nothing of this. He is listening to other voices 'singing, crying, stating, murmuring, things unintelligible, in his ear (p. 29). Like the characters of the trilogy later, he is following these inner voices away from such artificial puzzles to a confrontation with the true mysteries of the universe.

After Watt gets off the train at the station near Knott's house, he is seen walking along the road in the moonlight by Lady McCann, a woman of 'catholic and military' traditions, who lives in the neighborhood. Like the others before, she is both intrigued and vaguely annoyed by Watt's unusual appearance. 'Faithful to the spirit of her cavalier ascendants,' she indignantly throws a stone at this vagabond who is defiling the public road with his singularity:

'And it is to be supposed [that is, from the conventional Christian point of view of a person like Lady McCann] that God, always favorable to the McCanns . . . guided her hand, for the stone fell on Watt's hat and struck it from his head, to the ground' (p. 32). The Christian God, object of intellectual puzzling for the theologians, is a tribal deity for the lay believer.

Watt, who has long since grown accustomed to the indignities society inflicts on those who do not conform to its mores, simply picks up his hat and continues on his way to Knott's house. A little later, growing tired, he lies down in a ditch for a few minutes, although he knows that 'he must . . . move on again.' He is being driven on by a dimly felt necessity toward the revelation of nothingness that awaits him. As he lies there looking up at the moon, symbol again of time's inexorableness and repetitiousness— 'if there were two things Watt disliked, one was the moon, and the other was the sun' (p. 33)—he hears once more the chorus of voices, this time singing a descant on the number 52.142857142857142 . . . , a surd obtained by dividing the number of days in the year by the number of days in the week.[3] Representing the disharmony between sidereal time and man's calendar, this number symbolizes the inability of any human system of thought to describe adequately the reality of the universe. The song goes on further to describe the cyclical curve of human life as 'blooming . . . drooping . . . withered . . . forgotten' (p. 34). Here in miniature, contained in this song, is the picture of life that will comprise the 'quite useless wisdom' Watt will have 'so dearly won' by the time he finishes his quest.

When Watt leaves the conventional world behind, he leaves behind those who believe or claim to believe in the traditional God and enters a world in which a succession of servants devoutly serve an absurd parody of God. Those who come to Knott approach his house, as Watt does, 'with confidence and with awe' (p. 36) in the expectancy that there 'the first dawn' (p. 40) will break in which they will see revealed some ultimate meaning that will make sense of their lives. Actually Knott, as his name obliquely suggests, is nothing. But 'the only way one can speak of nothing is to speak of it as though it were something, just as the only way one can speak of God is to speak of him as though he were a man' (p. 77). To a person seeking the meaning of life, even if there is no such meaning, that meaning will appear to be something, and it will also appear to be awesome and quasi-divine, at least until its real emptiness is seen.

It might be appropriate to describe at this point the manner in which the story is being presented to the reader, since there are others besides Watt who are concerned with it and who are apparently seeking an important meaning in it. The account of Watt's experiences in Knott's house is being related by a person named Sam, to whom Watt told the story while he and Sam were copatients in what appears to be a mental hospital. Sam's story in turn is being presented to us by an editor, who occasionally points out gaps in Sam's manuscript (see pp. 238 and 241). There is much to suggest the idea that Watt's story may have only a very loose relationship to actual experiences. Sam says, for example, that Watt told him the story in a low, rapid monotone which was difficult to understand and that much of what he said 'by the rushing wind was carried away, and lost for ever' (p. 156). And as Watt went on in the desultory narration, which took place during increasingly infrequent intervals, Watt's speech came gradually to involve more and more convoluted constructions in which he inverted the order of the words in his sentences, the order of the letters in the words, the order of the sentences in the periods, and so on. This of course made the whole story very difficult for Sam even to follow, let alone record accurately. And the fact that both participants in the conversations were evidently mad makes the correspondence of the story to external reality extremely problematic. This is not, however, what is important. What matters is that the story of the quest for meaning seems important enough both to Watt and to Sam to be worth telling and writing down. There may never have been a real Knott, or the real Knott may have been a quite ordinary person magnified to semidivine status by the imagination of a servant on the edge of insanity. What is really important is simply what Knott represents in the story. To those driven mad by the need for a meaning, Knott is the meaninglessness, the nothingness, at the heart of the universe.

According to the story, all those who come to Knott's house, and there appears to be an endless succession of them, come with the same awe and the same expectancy and eventually leave with the same disillusionment. When Watt arrives, he is greeted by another servant, Arsene, who, now that Watt is there to replace him, is about to leave. Before going, Arsene kindly describes something of what Watt will find in Knott's house. Still more kindly, however, since he himself has already suffered the ultimate disappointment, Arsene does not tell Watt all that he will find : 'Not that I have told you all that I know, for I have not, being now a good-natured man . . . and indulgent towards the dreams of middle age, which were my dreams' (p. 62). The course he predicts for Watt resembles that of Dante in the *Purgatorio* and *Paradiso*. It consists of a long, slow ascent through specified labors which will eventually lead him up the first-floor stairs to the vision of Knott. These labors are 'of . . . exceptional fruitfulness' because in doing them the laborer comes to understand that 'he is working not merely for Mr Knott in person, and for Mr Knott's establishment, but also, and indeed chiefly, for himself' (p. 41). The goal of this work is that the one performing it will come to accept the tasks not as imposed from without but as voluntary, that he will come to accept Knott's will as his own. The labors of the spirits ascending the mountain of purgatory have a similar purpose; Dante's Piccarda explains in the *Paradiso* that the bliss of the soul in heaven depends on his developing a whole-hearted acceptance of God's will : '*E'n la sua volontade è nostra pace*' ('Our peace is in His will,' *Paradiso*, III 85). When the servant of Knott can accept his work in a similar identification of his own will with Knott's, then, like a soul in paradise, 'calm and glad he witnesses and is witnessed' (p. 42), and he takes his place among the succession of servants 'eternally turning about Mr Knott in tireless love' (p. 62).

This, at least, is the somewhat rosy picture Arsene paints for Watt. Since he has himself passed through this experience into disillusionment with the whole matter of Knott and his house and servants, Arsene could undoubtedly tell Watt much more that would correct this exaggerated impression of calmness, freedom, and 'tireless love,' but he has also learned that 'it is useless not to seek, not to want' (p. 44), because the compulsion to know would make the seeker go through the experience just the same. Arsene's conclusion from this is that if one is going to have to seek anyway, however vain he knows the search to be, then 'the nearest' one will 'ever get to felicity' is 'to hunger, thirst, lust, every day afresh and every day in vain' (p. 44). Murphy had worked hard to rid himself of all desires, and his moderate, though not complete, success in that endeavor appeared to give him a certain superiority over people like Neary, who was always scratching himself 'out of one itch into the next.' From the point of view of Arsene's deeper understanding of human nature, Neary's way would actually be preferable to Murphy's. Murphy had hoped for escape from all desire and from the life that desire held one to; Arsene knows that there is no escape, that life will carry one along even if one knows it is leading nowhere. Constantly renewed desire and hope, however futile and illusory, can help make the inevitable a little less boring.

Although Watt, like all his predecessors, eventually becomes disillusioned with Knott, Knott does for a while appear distinctly Godlike to him. Knott's house looks to Watt as if it has been in existence virtually since the beginning of time : '. . . as it was now, so it had been in the beginning, and so it would remain to the end, in all essential respects . . .' (p. 131), a paraphrase of the Christian formula describing God's eternality. Knott is served by 'an infinity of servants' (p. 133), who succeed each other according to a 'pre-established arbitrary' (p. 134) in a 'chain stretching from the long dead to the far unborn.' All of these men come to Knott seeking a haven. Knott himself never comes or goes, nor does he seem to share the needs that bring others to him : 'except, one, not to need, and, two, a witness to his not needing, Knott needed nothing, as far as Watt could see' (p. 202). In this, Knott resembles the God of Christianity, but the traditional God is supposed to be capable of existing even without the worshipers that He has for some mysterious reason wished to create. Knott, on the other hand, who knows nothing of himself (p. 203), is said to need witnesses 'that he might not cease.' He seems, therefore, to be the embodiment merely of the idea of God or of some sort of Absolute. His only reality is as a mental fiction in the mind of the person seeking him. To the person who finally sees through this illusion, Knott is not.

The process of arriving at this ultimate disillusionment is a slow and painful one. Contrary to Arsene's generously optimistic prediction, Watt never comes to feel 'calm and free and glad' (p. 135). He is tormented during all his time in Knott's house by a long series of problematic, brain-teasing incidents 'of great formal brilliance and indeterminable purport' (p. 74). He had never been especially bothered by problems of this sort before; until this time he 'had lived, miserably it is true, among face values all his adult life' (p. 73). In Knott's house, however, 'the fragility of the outer meaning' gradually becomes clearer to Watt than it had ever been before, and he is thus driven deeper and deeper into the swamp of meaninglessness to try to find a reality that constantly eludes him.

Typical of the puzzles that tease Watt is that of the piano tuners. Their name is Gall, and they claim to be father and son, although 'there was no family likeness between the two, as far as Watt could make out' (p. 70). The elder is blind 'like so many members of his profession,' but it is actually the younger who does the tuning. The strings of the piano are 'in flitters,' and almost all of the hammers and their corresponding dampers have been eaten by mice.

> The piano is doomed, in my opinion, said the younger.
> The piano-tuner also, said the elder.
> The pianist also, said the younger [p. 72].

This incident is said to have been typical 'in the sense that it was not ended, when it was past, but continued to unfold, in Watt's head, from beginning to end, over and over again' (p. 72). Watt cannot figure out what the relationship between the two Galls really is, whether they are really father and son or whether they are stepfather and stepson, whether the older is teaching the younger his trade or whether the younger simply takes the older on his rounds with him. He cannot figure out what they have to do with Knott or what their dialogue has to do with anything. As he goes over and over the incident, its meaning becomes more and more obscure, and yet he cannot free himself from 'the need to think that such and such a thing had happened then, the need to be able to say . . . Yes, I remember, that is what happened then' (p. 74). Eventually he will come to realize that the real problem was not so much that he did not know what had happened as that 'nothing had happened, that a thing that was nothing had happened, with the utmost formal distinctness, and that it continued to happen . . . inexorably to unroll its phases' (p. 76). This, however, is the hard won 'useless wisdom' he arrives at at the end of his stay. In the meantime he has to go through a long period of trying 'to elicit something from nothing' (p. 77) by 'foisting a meaning there where no meaning appeared.'

As time goes on, Watt finds that it is not only unusual and obviously puzzling incidents like that of the Galls that can embroil him in their 'unintelligible intricacies.' Even the most ordinary things become problematic to him. One of Mr Knott's pots, for example, comes to seem an inscrutable mystery : '. . . it was not a pot, the more he looked, the more he reflected, the more he felt sure of that, that it was not a pot at all. It resembled a pot, it was almost a pot, but it was not a pot of which one could say, Pot, pot, and be comforted' (p. 81). Nor is it a pot of which one could say it is not a pot, and be comforted : '. . . it was just this hairbreadth departure from the nature of a true pot that so excruciated Watt. For if the approximation had been less close, then Watt would have been less anguished.' As it is, all he can do is keep puzzling over and over the pot, never able to pin it down.

This is the basic human predicament in *Watt*, as in all of Beckett's novels. Reality, like the proverbial carrot on the end of a stick, torments one with its apparent closeness and yet always remains just beyond one's grasp. Watt attains a virtually heroic understanding of this situation when he comes to realize that reality itself will always be beyond his reach and that the most he can hope for is that he will at times be able to 'evolve, from the meticulous phantoms that beset him, a hypothesis proper to disperse them' (p. 78). A hypothesis can never describe reality, but it can sometimes set one's mind at rest temporarily. This rest can rarely be more than temporary, however, because to still the questioning mind effectively, the hypothesis has to appear to be true, and in most cases its falsehood will eventually become so evident that it will have to be replaced with another hypothesis, which in turn will eventually have to be replaced with yet another. Watt had previously understood this matter dimly—'For to explain had always been to exorcize, for Watt' (p. 78)[4]—but in Knott's house he comes to understand fully for the first time that there will always be an unbridgeable gap between the word and the thing, between explanation and reality. The hellish thing about this understanding—and this is probably what finally drives Watt mad —is that to be effective an explanation must have one's total, even if only temporary, belief. Exorcism operates by means of self-imposed illusions, and as Watt develops a clearer and clearer understanding of the real meaninglessness of the universe, such self-deception becomes increasingly difficult.

C

In the earlier stages of his stay in Knott's house, Watt is still
able to perform exorcisms of this sort, as when, in explaining the
series of dogs that are always available to eat Knott's left-over food,
he makes 'a pillow of old words' (p. 117) to rest his head on. But
as his stay goes on, more and more perplexing puzzles beset him,
leading finally to the ultimate unknowable, Knott himself. His first
glimpses of Knott, before he ascends to the first floor where he
is with Knott constantly, are not 'face to face' (p. 146), echoing
I Corinthians 13, 'but as it were in a glass' (p. 147). Even seeing
Knott dimly in this manner, Watt can tell that he is 'seldom the
same figure, from one glance to the next.' Later when he sees him
directly, he finds that there is nothing definite about him at all,
that he changes his entire appearance continually : 'For one day
Mr Knott would be tall, fat, pale and dark, and the next thin, small,
flushed and fair, and the next sturdy, middlesized, yellow and
ginger, and the next small, fat, pale and fair and the next middlesized, flushed, thin and ginger' and so on and so on (p. 209). During
all the time Watt has been working for Knott, Knott has been
the principal object of his curiosity, but when he finally sees him,
he learns only that nothing can be known of him. Little as he
could understand the other features of Knott's house, he remains
'in particular ignorance' regarding 'the nature of Mr Knott himself'
(p. 199).

Finally, after Watt has had plenty of time to savor the un-
intelligibility of Knott and of his house, another servant, named
Micks, comes to replace him as he had replaced Arsene. Time
continually brings new initiates to go through the experience of
disillusionment. In this work as in Beckett's other novels, the
patterns of time are circular. Change is constant, but the basic
situation remains the same : '. . . as it was now, so it had been
in the beginning, and so it would remain to the end, in all
essential respects . . . only the face changing . . . even as . . . Mr
Knott's face ever slowly changed' (p. 131). Just as the servants
come and go, so it is suggested—in the Addenda—that perhaps
'Mr Knott too was serial, in a vermicular series' (p. 253). Time,
which continually brings new questers, continually provides them
with new embodiments of nothing to seek, but the quest remains
always the same.

Nor do the cycles of time come to a stop even for the individuals
who complete the quest. There is no absolutely final disillusionment;

there is only one disillusionment after another. Like the flies in the window of the railroad station waiting room, 'exicted to new efforts by yet another dawn' (p. 236), Watt will keep trying futilely over and over to reach the light. When Arsene was leaving after completing his own stay in Knott's house, he said, 'If I could begin it all over again, knowing what I know now, the result would be the same. . . . And if I could begin it all over again a hundred times . . . the result would always be the same, and the hundredth life as the first, and the hundred lives as one' (p. 47). In actuality, one does begin it all over again, a hundred times and more; man is doomed by his very nature to the endless quest for a meaning that is not there. As Watt leaves with his newly found 'useless wisdom,' he sees on the way to the station a vague figure ahead of him on the road. He is fascinated by it because he cannot tell whether it is the figure 'of a man, or that of a woman, or that of a priest, or that of a nun' (p. 225). Intrigued, he waits 'with impatience' (p. 226) for the figure to approach. He does not know why he cares what the figure is, and he even feels that it is 'greatly to be deplored' that he cares, but nothing is able to prevent his 'for ever falling into this old error, this error of the old days when, lacerated with curiosity, in the midst of substance shadowy he stumbled' (p. 227). After teasing Watt to such agitated impatience that he shakes with all his might the wicket he is leaning on, the figure grows fainter and finally disappears.

The wisdom gained in Knott's house does not lead to freedom or even to indifference. Even the knowledge that certainty can never be found does not still the questioning mind. The only progress is toward a deeper appreciation of the futility of the compulsive quest. And the more one understands both the futility and the compulsive character of man's need to know, the more painful becomes the life dominated by it. This is what Arsene meant when he told Watt about the three modes of laughter, the bitter, the hollow, and the mirthless :

The bitter laugh laughs at that which is not good, it is the ethical laugh. The hollow laugh laughs at that which is not true, it is the intellectual laugh. . . . But the mirthless laugh . . . is the laugh of laughs, the *risus purus*, the laugh laughing at the laugh . . . the laugh that laughs . . . at that which is unhappy [p. 48].

Arsene describes them as corresponding to 'successive excoriations of the understanding.' Progress in understanding of the basic situation of life is progress toward the mirthless laugh, toward the realization that human life is hopelessly unhappy, that man, torn between disillusionment and the need for illusions, is condemned to perpetual frustration.

This is the 'useless wisdom' Watt finally arrives at, and just how useless it is will be demonstrated fully in the trilogy, which examines the entire process of disillusionment from beginnings much more naïve than those of Watt, to understanding and frustration much deeper than those Watt reaches.

When Watt leaves Knott's house, he encounters at the railroad station a group of people similar to those at the beginning of the book. One of them is even the Lady McCann who threw the rock at him the night he arrived. They are people whose shallow trust in the traditional evasions has insulated them from the kind of knowledge Watt has to suffer. They can understand neither the mirthlessness of man's basic frustration, nor the hollowness of that which is not true, nor even the bitterness of that which is ethically evil. Finding Watt on the floor after they themselves have accidentally knocked him down, Mr Nolan and Mr Gorman, concerned only with the respectability of their railroad, try to rouse this apparent vagabond by throwing a bucket of water over him. The bucket slips and injures him : 'Blood now perfused the slime' (p. 241). As we know from the beginning of the book, even a minor injury is serious to Watt because he has 'a poor healing skin' (p. 32) so that a wound once opened is open 'never again to close, never, never again to close.' But Gorman and Nolan are 'not alarmed.' They sell Watt a ticket to the end of the line and thus get rid of him. The book ends with the railroad men rejoicing complacently in the beauty of the sunrise :

All the same, said Mr Gorman, life isn't such a bad old bugger. He raised high his hands and spread them out, in a gesture of worship. He then replaced them in the pockets, of his trousers. When all is said and done, he said.

. . . . . .

And they say there is no God, said Mr Case.
All three laughed heartily at this extravagance [pp. 245-46].

Watt maintains a strict distinction between those who face the chaotic reality of the universe and those who hide from this vision behind the traditional illusions of their society. Beckett's next major work, the trilogy, takes a different, more comprehensive approach to the portrait of human nature. Instead of separating mankind into those who face reality and those who do not, the trilogy shows the gradual breakdown of the traditional illusions and the slow dawning of the true vision in a series of characters who represent all levels of human experience. Moran, in *Molloy*, starts out as a bourgeois as conventional as Hackett and the Nixons, as Catholic as Lady McCann, and as punctilious in his concern with the duties of his profession as the three railroad men were in *Watt*. The person Moran is seeking, on the other hand, and whom he comes more and more to resemble as his journey progresses, is a vagabond like Watt who has explored the traditional fields of human knowledge and has become disillusioned with them all. The subsequent volumes of the trilogy carry their protagonists deeper and deeper into the realization of the inadequacy of all human attempts to understand the universe.

After finishing *Watt* and before undertaking the trilogy, which involved a shift from the English language to French, Beckett made some initial experiments with French[5] in a few minor works. These were the unpublished novel 'Mercier et Camier,'[6] and four stories 'La Fin,' 'L'Expulsé,' 'Le Calmant,' and 'Premier amour,' written in approximately that order.[7] Of these, the only ones published were 'La Fin,' (titled 'Suite' when it first appeared[8]), 'L'Expulsé,' and 'Le Calmant.' The three were published together by the Éditions de Minuit, Paris, in 1955 in the collection *Nouvelles et Textes pour rien*, where an editor's note says they were written in 1945. They appear in *Nouvelles* in the order 'L'Expulsé,' 'Le Calmant,' and 'La Fin.' In 1967 these were published in English translation as the *Stories* of *Stories and Texts for nothing*. There they are called 'The Expelled,' 'The Calmative,' and 'The End.'[9]

Like the volumes of the trilogy, these three stories are narrated in the first person. The speaker is similar enough in each of the three to make them appear to constitute a single portrait. If this is in fact the case, then the portrait is of a person who has a number of interesting similarities to the characters of the trilogy. Like Malone and Molloy, the speaker is a vagabond. Like Moran too, however, he seems to have come from a distinctly bourgeois back-

ground and to have felt some attachment to it at one time. When
he is thrown out of what appears to be his family's house in 'The
Expelled,' he crosses the street to get a last look at it, exclaims on
its beauty, and tells how he had always admired its large, impressive door and how for years he had doted on the geraniums in the
window boxes.

Like most of the characters of the trilogy after him, he is very
attached to his possessions, especially to his hat. It was given to
him by his father, and he speaks of it as though it had been
predestined just for him. The hat is mentioned several times in
the course of the three stories. It seems to be to him a sort of
symbol of his identity or of the continuity of his experience. He
keeps it fastened to his coat by means of a string so as not to lose
it, and he is very disturbed when the attendants of some sort of
rest home or asylum take it and his coat away and burn them
at the beginning of 'The End' and give him those of a dead man.
This episode suggests the very similar one in *Malone Dies* in which
Malone's character MacMann makes such an outcry about the
loss of his hat in almost the same circumstances that his nurse
finally goes and retrieves it from the dung-heap for him. Molloy,
too, is disturbed when Lousse's valet takes away his hat and clothes
in *Molloy*, and at times the language he uses in speaking of it
makes it seem to be very much a symbol to him of his identity :
'I took off my hat and looked at it. It is fastened, to my buttonhole,
at all seasons, by a long lace. I am still alive then' (*Molloy*, p. 16).

At the beginning of 'The Calmative,' as the narrator talks about
his intention to tell stories in order to calm himself, he sounds very
much like Malone at the beginning of *Malone Dies*, and the fact
that he speaks of himself as already dead makes him sound like
the Unnamable. The story he tells is distinctly suggestive of those
in the trilogy in that the world he describes is one in which all
men are solitary : 'All the mortals I saw were alone and as if sunk in
themselves' (p. 38). This is an anticipation of the world Malone
describes in which people heading home after work in the evening
avoid each other as they pursue their solitary paths : 'And even
those who know themselves condemned, at the outset, to the same
direction . . . take leave of one another and part . . . with some
polite excuse, or without a word . . .' (*Malone*, p. 56). Solitude is
a subject that the early novels of Beckett touched on relatively
briefly but which the trilogy develops into a major theme. The

solitude of the narrator of the *Stories* and of the world he wanders through or which he tells stories about is an important step toward the trilogy.

Another important step in the transition from the English novels to the trilogy is the experimentation in the initial French writings with a simpler and more colloquial tone. The English works were narrated in the third person in a tone of detached irony and of playful pedantry. The language was purposely a little stilted. The *Stories* use colloquial tone in connection with first person narration, which means that the irony, though still present, is more indirect and less mockingly fastidious, and which has the great advantage that it can communicate not only the folly of the characters, but also their anguish. This is the technique that Beckett was later to use so effectively in all of his subsequent fiction through *How It Is*.

'Mercier et Camier' uses the older third person technique of narration, but its language, too, is simpler than that of the English works. Its importance, however, is less as a precursor of the trilogy than of the plays. It is about the travels of a couple of old men who rather closely resemble Vladimir and Estragon of *Waiting for Godot*. Camier, like Gogo, is short and fat, and Mercier, like Didi, is tall and thin. Much of the dialogue between the two has also been reproduced almost exactly in the same play.[10]

CHAPTER V

The Structure of the Trilogy

The three volumes of Beckett's trilogy are narrated by four principal characters : Molloy, Moran, Malone, and the Unnamable. The first volume, *Molloy,* is divided into two sections of equal length. Molloy is the narrator of the first section, Moran of the second.

Molloy writes his story for reasons that are not clear to him. He only knows that he is in his mother's room writing in her bed. There is a man who comes and leaves money in return for pages, although Molloy says he does not write for money. He assumes that his mother has died and that he has taken her place. He mentions that he may have a son (Moran?) somewhere. At the beginning of his story Molloy speaks of seeing two travellers, A and C,[1] who meet momentarily outside a town and then proceed on their separate ways, A back to the town, C on alone into the distance. The vision of C so old and solitary apparently arouses feelings of loneliness in Molloy, because he decides suddenly to go visit his mother. Finding his bicycle by the road, he sets out.

At one point he is detained by the police, who question him as to his identity. It is only with some difficulty that Molloy can remember his own name, and he cannot remember the name of his town at all. Not until Moran's narrative is the reader told that Molloy's town is named Bally. Proceeding on his journey after being released by the police, Molloy accidentally runs over and kills a dog belonging to a woman named Lousse. Lousse, wishing Molloy to take the place of her dog, detains him. Finally, after an unspecified length of time, Molloy escapes from her house, though without his bicycle. Since one of his legs is stiff, he proceeds on crutches. Occasionally he interrupts his journey to lie down and relax, but always the need to go on reasserts itself. Gradually his good leg stiffens, and his bad leg becomes worse. Toward the end of his story, lost in a forest, he can only crawl. At the very end he hears a gong and finds himself at the edge of the forest. Since Moran too hears a gong, the gong with which his cook, Martha, calls him to dinner, it may be that Molloy's journey has terminated in Moran's backyard.

If it is in fact Moran's dinner gong that Molloy hears, then he arrives at Moran's house on the very day Moran is ordered by Youdi, through his agent Gaber, to pursue Molloy. Youdi's orders also include that Moran is to take his son with him on the journey. Dutifully, but reluctantly, Moran sets out with his son in search of Molloy. He dislikes having to leave the comfort of his home.

Before Moran set out he felt a sharp pain in his knee. During the journey he feels it again several times. Gradually his leg becomes stiff. After he has had a fight with his son, who subsequently abandons him, and has given up the quest for Molloy entirely, he receives orders from Youdi, through Gaber again, to return home. The return takes all winter. By the time he arrives at his home he can hardly walk. Perhaps he has found Molloy by becoming assimilated to him. Writing about all this, Moran says that he no longer acts out of fear of Youdi, but in obedience to an inner voice. Apparently directed by this voice, he decides to set out again, on crutches. 'Perhaps I shall meet Molloy,' he says.

Malone strongly resembles Molloy. He too is an old man writing alone in a room in bed. The difference is that he does not claim to write about his own life. He makes up a fictitious character whom he first calls Sapo, later changing his name to Macmann. *Malone Dies* could hardly be called an eventful novel. Malone simply tells stories to pass the time while he is waiting to die. Even the life of his invented character is relatively quiet. As the boy Sapo, the character does very little. The most entertaining part of Sapo's boyhood, for the reader, is the time he spends with the family of Big Lambert, a slaughterer of pigs. After Sapo's name is changed to Macmann, his life becomes more lively, especially at the end when, as an old man, he enters an insane asylum, the House of St John of God. In the asylum Macmann lives in a room like those of Molloy and Malone. The most interesting episode concerns a grotesque love affair between Macmann and his nurse, Moll. The narrative ends in fragments which one feels must be the last gasps of the dying Malone.

The Unnamable seems to be the sort of person Malone might have become after death. He feels that he has died, but can not understand why death has not brought him extinction. He has no idea where he is. Vague figures pass before him. For a moment he thinks one of them may be Malone, but then wonders if it might not be Molloy wearing Malone's hat. For lack of anything else to do, and to relieve his loneliness, he begins to tell stories.

The first story is about Mahood, a person with one leg who travels around the world, finally returning to orbit about his family. The second is about a person named Worm who has no limbs, only a trunk, and who lives in a jar,[2] tended by a woman named Madeleine or Marguerite—the Unnamable is not sure exactly which. This woman uses Worm as a signpost for her restaurant near the stockyards. As he proceeds in the narration, the Unnamable gradually becomes convinced that the stories are being told not by him but by a voice which is independent of his control. He has difficulty distinguishing between himself and the characters of the stories. It is as if the stories were lives the voice wanted to live. He would like the voice to go silent, but he has no idea what could bring this about. As the novel continues, the Unnamable becomes increasingly confused as to who he is and longs with increasing desperation to escape into unconsciousness. By the last page he is in total despair. He only knows that he is compelled by the voice to go on thinking and talking, endlessly : '. . . you must go on, I can't go on, I'll go on.'

Perhaps the first problem that occurs to any reader of Beckett's trilogy is that of the relations among the main characters. The question is whether these are totally distinct from each other or whether they are the same character at different stages of a process of development. The various narrators are connected by a number of obvious similarities. They have a great many personal characteristics in common including their physical deficiencies, their clothing, their personalities and preoccupations as well as their activities, especially those of traveling and writing. There are also continuities of environment that tend to tie them together, such as the forests they journey through, the rooms and beds they live in, the objects they come across during their lifetimes, such as crutches, bicycles, sucking-stones, kniferests, and the like, and the similar people they meet or are concerned with. They all have Irish surnames, except for the Unnamable, and they seem to share a Roman Catholic religious background, attested to by various pious or mock-pious references to Roman Catholic devotions, such as the Angelus and the stations of the cross, and to the seasons of the ecclesiastical calendar.

These similarities, however, are relatively superficial. They show only that the characters of the trilogy have a sort of family resemblance. There are also numerous suggestions recurring throughout the three volumes that there is an even closer relationship among the narrators : that certain ones among them may be the fictional creations of one or more of the other characters or that each of them represents one level of consciousness within a single multileveled person. Molloy, for example, refers in one place to somebody laughing somewhere and adds, 'Inside me too someone was laughing' (*Molloy*, p. 33), which suggests that to Molloy it seems as if there is another level within him which is sufficiently distinct from his own conscious personality that it should be referred to as 'someone.' And Malone says almost the same thing rather early in his narrative when he says, 'My concern is not with me, but with another, far beneath me' (*Malone*, p. 19), and when he goes on to say a few lines later on the same page that he feels 'behind my closed eyes, other eyes close.'

Moran, too, shares this feeling that there is some deeper level within him, but in his case he explicitly identifies or associates it with the Molloy he is to seek. When he first attempts to think about Molloy he does it by lapsing into a dreamlike state and looking within himself : 'For it was only by transferring it to this atmosphere . . . that I could venture to consider the work I had on hand. For where Molloy could not be, nor Moran either for that matter, there Moran could bend over Molloy' (*Molloy*, p. 152). And the reality Moran attributes to Molloy tends to be a mental reality—'Perhaps I had invented him, I mean found him ready made in my head' (*Molloy*, pp. 152-53)—though in one place (p. 157) he distinguishes between the inner Molloy and 'the man of flesh and blood somewhere awaiting me.'

When Molloy says, 'Yes, let me cry out, this time, then another time perhaps, then perhaps a last time' (p. 33), it sounds as if he dimly suspects that he will speak 'another time' at a deeper level with the voice of Malone and then 'perhaps' a last time with the voice of the Unnamable.[3] It may be that Molloy is telling the story of his own life 'this time' and that after death he recovers consciousness as Malone. This possibility is suggested by a passage in *Malone* on page 45 : 'There is naturally another possibility that does not escape me . . . and that is that I am dead already and that all continues more or less as when I was not. Perhaps I expired in the forest, or even earlier.' This reminds the reader of Molloy in the forest. A few pages later Malone seems to have other memories of a life that resembles what we know of Molloy's : '. . . it sometimes seems to me I did get born and had a long life and met Jackson and wandered in the towns, the woods and wildernesses and tarried by the seas . . .' (p. 52). Molloy never said that he knew a Jackson, but the rest of the description could fit him.

Nevertheless, this evidence is far from conclusive; it could just as easily be that Malone is remembering a previous life as a Malone who only resembled Molloy. It could even be that all the lives up to the end of *Malone* are fictions told by Malone, who subsequently finds himself to be the Unnamable after his own death.

Malone does seem to have premonitions of the Unnamable as that which will continue after he dies. At least this seems to be what Malone is talking about in one of the more obscure passages toward the end of his volume :

> Weary with my weariness, white last moon, sole regret, not even. To be dead, before her, on her, with her, and turn, dead on dead, about poor mankind, and never have to die any more, from among the living. Not even, not even that. . . . And one day, soon, soon, one earthlit night, beneath the earth, a dying being will say, like me, in the earthlight, Not even, not even that, and die, without have been able to find a regret [*Malone*, pp. 93-94].

The 'dying being' who will go on talking 'beneath the earth' could be the Unnamable, who refers to a past life 'above in the island' (*Unnamable*, p. 54), thereby situating himself beneath the earth apparently. When Malone likens himself to the moon turning 'dead on dead, about poor mankind,' it sounds like a premonition of his condition in the next volume rotating in orbit around the

Unnamable: 'Malone is there. Of his mortal liveliness little trace remains. He passes before me at doubtless regular intervals' (*Unnamable*, p. 5).

There are also various suggestions that the one permanent personality behind all the narrators and speaking through all of them with a single voice is the Unnamable. For example, when Malone says, 'The forms are many in which the unchanging seeks relief from its formlessness' (*Malone*, p. 21), and when he says of his own life, 'I mean the business of Malone (since that is what I am called now)' (p. 48), he sounds like the Unnamable trying to retain his sense of the distinction between himself and the characters he is talking about or who are talking through him. A passage of similar import also occurs in *Molloy* in which Molloy, commenting on his story, says, 'If I go on long enough calling that my life I'll end up by believing it' (p. 71). This sounds very like Malone's 'I mean the business of Malone (since that is what I am called now).' In both these statements a deeper level within, possibly the Unnamable, seems to be distinguishing between itself and the forms, Molloy and Malone, 'in which the unchanging seeks relief from its formlessness.'

The Unnamable shares with the other characters their preoccupation with levels, but in his case it takes on a slightly different form since each of the others felt a fairly definite sense of a level within himself deeper than his conscious personality. The Unnamable, on the other hand, starts with the idea that he is or should be the deepest of all levels and that there is no reason to suppose any other depths beyond him. Still, even though he wants to believe this, he feels so uncertain about everything that he feels apprehensive about this also:

Are there other pits deeper down? To which one accedes by mine? Stupid obsession with depth. Are there other places set aside for us and this one where I am, with Malone, merely their narthex? I thought I had done with preliminaries. . . . Is not this rather the place where one finishes vanishing? [*Unnamable*, p. 6].

The same attitude is seen a few pages later when the Unnamable tries to understand the manner in which Malone is orbiting about him 'like a planet about its sun.' He wants to think of himself as the sun or fixed point of this cosmos, which would mean he himself was the basic reality or deepest level, but he also recognizes that there is no necessary reason to suppose this : 'It is equally possible, I do not deny it, that I too am in perpetual motion, accompanied by Malone, as the earth by its moon' (p. 9).

The fact that it is Malone who is seen orbiting the Unnamable makes it appear that there is some special relationship between the two, and just as there were hints in Malone's narrative that he might be a continuation or afterlife of Molloy, so there are also suggestions in the text of *The Unnamable* that the title-character may be a post mortem state of Malone. The Unnamable's statement about a 'life above in the island' was mentioned above as possibly referring to an earlier life as Malone. This possibility as well as the possibility that the Unnamable may have been incarnate in several other characters of the trilogy is suggested in many places in the last volume. His narrative opens with an expression of utter bewilderment as to who he is and where he is, and the first possibility he mentions as an explanation of his situation sounds as if it could refer to previous lives :

> Can it be that one day . . . I simply stayed in, in where, instead of going out, in the old way. . . . Perhaps that is how it began. You think you are simply resting, the better to act when the time comes, or for no reason, and you soon find yourself powerless ever to do anything again [*Unnamable*, p. 3].

When he says a few pages later, 'I have been here, ever since I began to be, my appearances elsewhere having been put in by other parties' (p. 7), he is trying to deny this possibility and to fix his identity as that of his present self, but the manner in which he phrases his denial, referring, for example, to 'my appearances elsewhere,' seems to affirm what it denies and to betray a division within the speaker's own mind.

This possibility of previous incarnations, as well as the Unnamable's ambiguous attitude toward the possibility, is further developed at a later point when the Unnamable is trying to maintain a distinction between himself and the current threat to his sense of identity, Mahood : 'Mahood. Before him there were others, taking themselves for me, it must be a sinecure handed down from

generation to generation, to judge by their family air' (p. 37). Three
lines later he refers to Worm, the 'billy in the bowl,' as 'my next
vice-exister.' But the real essence of the problem is enunciated most
clearly just a few lines further still :

> In the meantime it's Mahood, this caricature is he. What if we
> were one and the same after all, as he affirms, and I deny?
> And I been in the places where he says I have been, instead
> of having stayed on here, trying to take advantage of his absence
> to unravel my tangle? Here, in my domain, what is Mahood
> doing in my domain, and how does he get here? There I am
> launched again on the same old hopeless business, there we are
> face to face, Mahood and I, if we are twain, as I say we are.
> I never saw him, I don't see him, he has told me what he is
> like, what I am like, they have all told me that, it must be one
> of their principal functions [*Unnamable*, pp. 37-38].

Here it becomes clear that the problem of the relations among
the characters of the trilogy and of their possible continuity or
identity is inseparable from the problem of identity as such.
The Unnamable cannot even determine his own identity with
any confidence since he cannot distinguish between himself and
the characters that are being told about by a voice speaking through
him. Nor is the Unnamable the first character in the trilogy
to feel that personal identity is a problem. Molloy, for example,
says at one point that his 'sense of identity was wrapped in a
namelessness often hard to penetrate' (*Molloy*, p. 41), and
Malone in turn says that he does not know 'who I am, nor
where I am, nor if I am' (*Malone*, p. 52). The earlier characters,
however, do not connect the problem of identity with the voices
they hear or the stories they tell. When Malone says a few lines
later on the same page about his relation to Sapo, 'I slip into him,
I suppose in the hope of learning something,' he sounds for a
moment like the Unnamable, whose tendency to identify with
Mahood and Worm is a sort of slipping into them, but Malone
still thinks he is speaking with his own voice. There is no part of
the trilogy in which mention is not made of voices that speak
either to or through the characters. During the first two volumes,
though, the voices are thought of as definitely distinct from the
characters who hear them, even though they hear them within.
It is only in *The Unnamable* that the two themes of identity and

voices come to be seen as so closely connected that they amount in reality to two aspects of a single problem.

When the Unnamable first speaks of the voice, he describes it as an alien and hostile presence. Its particular type of hostility consists in its attempt to usurp his identity, so that even though he insists it is not his voice he sees it as coming from within him and filling him, and he acknowledges that there is no one else to whom it could belong :

> It issues from me, it fills me, it clamours against my walls, it is not mine, I can't stop it, I can't prevent it, from tearing me, racking me, assailing me. It is not mine, I have none, I have no voice and must speak, that is all I know, its round that I must revolve, of that I must speak, with this voice that is not mine, but can only be mine, since there is no one but me . . . [*Unnamable*, p. 26].

The manner in which the voice usurps his identity is made clearer a few pages later when he tells the reader about Basil, whose name he changes to Mahood, an action which in itself signifies the slipperiness of identity in this volume :

> Decidedly Basil is becoming important, I'll call him Mahood instead, I prefer that, I'm queer. It was he told me stories about me, lived in my stead, issued forth from me, came back to me, entered back into me, heaped stories on my head. . . . It is his voice which has often, always, mingled with mine, and sometimes drowned it completely [*Unnamable*, p. 29].

Here the voice is associated with a definite personality, in this case that of Mahood, and it is this personality that tries to occupy the identity of the Unnamable by filling him with its voice, telling 'me stories about me' and living 'in my stead.' This is supported by the fact that when Mahood's story is finally told, it is spoken by the Unnamable in the first person as though he were telling the story of his own life : 'Mahood himself nearly codded me more than once. I've been he an instant, hobbling through a nature which, it is only fair to say, was on the barren side. . . . Then I withdrew my adhesion . . .' (*Unnamable*, p. 39).

The story of Mahood continues in the first person. It is the story of a man with one leg who has been around the world on crutches and has returned to orbit about his family : 'At the particular moment I am referring to, I mean when I took myself for Mahood, I must have been coming to the end of a world tour. . . . In a word I was returning to the fold . . .' (*Unnamable*, pp. 40-41). The fold he returns to consists of his family and a house which is described as 'a small rotunda, windowless, but well furnished with loopholes.' For some reason he cannot proceed directly to them, but can only circle around them : 'So we turned, in our respective orbits, I without, they within' (p. 41). During all this, the Unnamable remains conscious of the subterfuges Mahood uses to make him think he is Mahood. For example, when the grandparents tell Mahood's children the story of his early life, the Unnamable calls this one of Mahood's tricks :

> In the evening, after supper, while my wife kept her eye on me, gaffer and gammer related my life history, to the sleepy children. Bedtime story atmosphere. That's one of Mahood's favourite tricks, to produce ostensibly independent testimony in support of my historical existence [*Unnamable*, pp. 42-43].

Another trick is to make him feel his existence more intensely by rendering it more uncomfortable : 'Mahood must have remarked that I remained sceptical, for he casually let fall that I was lacking not only a leg, but an arm also' (p. 46). When the story of Mahood finally ends, the Unnamable terminates it with :

> But enough of this nonsense. I was never anywhere but here, no one ever got me out of here. Enough of acting the infant who has been told so often how he was found under a cabbage that in the end he remembers the exact spot in the garden and the kind of life he led there before joining the family circle [*Unnamable*, p. 50].

He seems to think he is through with this invasion of his personality, but before long it begins again, though this time in a different form, that of Worm, a creature who has no arms or legs and who lives in a jar, tended by a woman named Marguerite or Madeleine who runs a restaurant near a slaughterhouse and uses Worm in his jar as a sign for her restaurant. Again the Unnamable identifies himself with the character being told about, and again the problem of identity is connected with the trouble he has distinguishing

between himself and the voice talking through him as if it were
his :

> Is there a single word of mine in all I say? No, I have no voice,
> in this matter I have none. That's one of the reasons why I
> confused myself with Worm. . . . But I don't say anything,
> I don't know anything, these voices are not mine, nor these
> thoughts, but the voices and thoughts of the devils who beset me.
> Who make me say that I can't be Worm, the inexpugnable. Who
> make me say that I am he perhaps, as they are. Who make me
> say that since I can't be he I must be he. That since I couldn't
> be Mahood, as I might have been, I must be Worm, as I cannot
> be [*Unnamable*, pp. 83-84].

As the Unnamable describes it at this point there are many voices.
Their purpose is to convince him somehow that one of the voices
is his own :

> That's to lull me, till I imagine I hear myself at last, to myself
> at last, that it can't be they, speaking thus, that it can only be
> I, speaking thus. Ah if I could only find a voice of my own,
> in all this babble, it would be the end of their troubles, and of
> mine [*Unnamable*, pp. 84-85].

For the Unnamable it seems that to be is to be spoken by a voice,
and if one of the voices could succeed in convincing him that
the words it is speaking are his and that the life it is recounting
is his own, he would then exist. As it is, however, he only hovers
between being and nonbeing, since he can neither identify completely with any of the voices nor totally dissociate himself from
them : 'Ah if only this voice could stop, this meaningless voice
which prevents you from being nothing, just barely prevents you
from being nothing and nowhere . . .' (pp. 116-17).

By this time it is clear that the question of the identity or
disparateness of the characters of the trilogy is one for which
there is no simple answer. Since the Unnamable cannot even find
his own voice among the voices of the characters speaking through
him, the whole issue of personal identity dissolves into meaninglessness. It is no more possible to say that the Unnamable is one with
the other characters or that he is the one constant personality behind
them all than it is to say that he is distinct from them. Nor is it

any more possible to say that any one of the characters is distinct from or identical with any of the others. For Beckett's trilogy, man is a vast enigma, unable to locate a definite sense of identity or even to feel confident of the very existence of a 'self' within him. It is probably for this reason that Beckett has constructed the work in such a way that although various possible interpretations of the relations among the characters are suggested, no one interpretation is ever allowed to establish itself to the exclusion of the others. The reality that the trilogy is describing—the reality of the human self—is too mysterious to be simplified, and to interpret it in too definite a way would be to falsify it. The most adequate conclusion would seem to be that all of the characters taken together constitute a composite portrait of man or of the human condition.

This idea is suggested in numerous passages throughout the three volumes. Molloy, for example, near the very beginning of his narrative, reflecting on his life and memories, says, 'People pass too, hard to distinguish from yourself. That is discouraging. So I saw A and C going slowly towards each other' (*Molloy*, p. 9), which makes Molloy himself and A and C, all three, seem to merge into a single figure. And when a few pages later Molloy describes C's anxiety, he makes C seem less an individual than a personification of man, acted upon by the forces common to all men :

Yes, he saw himself threatened, his body threatened, his reason threatened, and perhaps he was, perhaps they were. . . . I watched him recede, overtaken (myself) by his anxiety, at least by an anxiety which was not necessarily his, but of which as it were he partook [*Molloy*, p. 12].

Moran also tends to see the activities and concerns of men as the expression of their common humanity. Describing his concern with finding Molloy, for example, he thinks of it as a force common to all men and grounded in human nature :

For what I was doing I was doing neither for Molloy, who mattered nothing to me, nor for myself, of whom I despaired, but on behalf of a cause which, while having need of us to be accomplished, was in its essence anonymous, and would subsist, haunting the minds of men, when its miserable artisans should be no more [*Molloy*, pp. 156-57].

On the very first page of his account he had already said something
similar about how his son would someday go through the same
process : 'My son is sleeping. Let him sleep. The night will come
when he too, unable to sleep, will get up and go to his desk. I
shall be forgotten' (p. 125). Reflecting on his quest and on Molloy as
the goal of that quest, Moran thinks of mankind as one solid block
and of Molloy as interchangeable with any other person within
that block : 'There somewhere man is too, vast conglomerate of all
of nature's kingdoms, as lonely and as bound. And in that block
the prey is lodged and thinks himself a being apart. Anyone would
serve' (p. 151).

Malone in turn makes a similar statement about Macmann.
Having ceased talking about Macmann for a while to talk about
himself he returns to Macmann but feels somewhat uncertain that
the new Macmann is the same one he was describing earlier. He
concludes that it makes no difference, since all Macmanns are
alike :

> Can it be then that it is not the same Macmann at all, after all,
> in spite of the great resemblance (for those who know the power
> of the passing years), both physical and otherwise. It is true
> the Macmanns are legion in the island and pride themselves,
> what is more, with few exceptions, on having one and all, in
> the last analysis, sprung from the same illustrious ball. It is
> therefore inevitable they should resemble one another, now and
> then, to the point of being confused even in the minds of those
> who wish them well and would like nothing better than to tell
> between them. No matter, any old remains of flesh and spirit
> do, there is no sense in stalking people. So long as it is what is
> called a living being you can't go wrong, you have the guilty
> one [*Malone*, p. 88].

It should also be noted that the very name 'Macmann' would be
the Irish equivalent of 'son of man.'

Since the boundaries between individuals become generally
blurred in *The Unnamable* it can be said that the entire last volume
is permeated with the idea that each of the characters is interchangeable basically with any other and that each is consequently
representative of man as such. It may even be that the Unnamable
is called 'mankind' by Malone if a passage cited earlier from
Malone can in fact be taken as a premonition of the Unnamable :

'Weary with my weariness, white last moon. . . . To be dead, before her, on her, with her, and turn, dead on dead, about poor mankind' (p. 93).

An examination of the relations among the characters of the trilogy and of the manner in which together they make up a composite portrait of man would not be complete without some mention of the fact that actually the cast of characters cannot be limited only to Molloy, Moran, Malone, Macmann, the Unnamable, Mahood, and Worm. Many passages of the work mention Murphy, Watt, and other figures from earlier Beckett novels. The relations of the main characters of the trilogy extend beyond their own circle to an entire miniature universe of Beckett characters.

Mention of characters from other works by Beckett occurs at random throughout the three volumes of the trilogy. Molloy mentions only one, Watt, but when he does he expresses surprise that not everybody has heard of him : '. . . for they had never heard of Watt, just imagine that . . .' (*Molloy*, p. 103). It is probably significant that this reference to Watt does not occur in the correspondent place in the French text (pp. 116-17), which says only, *'car les chemins de fer étaient encore à l'état de projet.'* It is unlikely that Patrick Bowles, the titular translator, would have introduced such a change into the translation if it had not been the desire of Beckett himself, to whom the presence of Watt's name must have seemed important.

Moran mentions many of Beckett's earlier characters, and in this case the French and English texts agree. On page 188 he mentions Murphy, Watt, Mercier, and a certain Yerk as among those he has had to pursue before his present assignment to find Molloy, and toward the end of his journey he wonders : 'Would we all meet again in heaven one day, I, my mother, my son, his mother, Youdi, Gaber, Molloy, his mother, Yerk, Murphy, Watt, Camier and the rest?' (*Molloy*, p. 230). And Malone in turn speculates on the possibility that when he dies, 'it will be all over with the Murphys, Merciers, Molloys, Morans and Malones, unless it goes on beyond the grave' (*Malone*, p. 63).

As with many other themes, however, it is only in the final volume that this theme reaches its full complexity and is characteristically united with the problem of identity. On page 37 the Unnamable says, 'Mahood. Before him there were others, taking themselves for me, it must be a sinecure handed down from generation to generation, to judge by their family air.' It cannot be supposed that he is here referring only to Molloy, Moran, and Malone as the previous holders of the 'sinecure'; before making this statement he has already referred several times to other members of the Beckett universe. For example, as early as page 6 he says : 'To tell the truth I believe they are all here, at least from Murphy on, I believe we are all here.' On page 11 he speculates that two oblong shapes he sees colliding before him may be 'the pseudo-couple Mercier-Camier.' And on page 21 he includes Murphy in a list of characters he accuses of having usurped his identity : 'All these Murphys, Molloys and Malones do not fool me. They have made me waste my time, suffer for nothing, speak of them when, in order to stop speaking, I should have spoken of me and of me alone. . . .' Somewhat later he expresses the same idea again, mentioning Watt and Mercier : 'I am neither, I needn't say, Murphy, nor Watt, nor Mercier, nor—no, I can't even bring myself to name them, nor any of the others whose very names I forget, who told me I was they . . .' (p. 53).

Many similar statements from the last volume could be cited, but one later instance in particular should be mentioned because of its explicit association of this theme with that of the voice :

> . . . he thinks he's caught me, he feels me in him, then he says I, as if I were he, or in another, let us be just, then he says Murphy, or Molloy, I forget, as if I were Malone, but their day is done . . . it's always he who speaks, Mercier never spoke, Moran never spoke, I never spoke, I seem to speak, that's because he says I as if he were I . . . [*Unnamable*, pp. 163-64].

The idea that there is a single voice that has told the stories of earlier Beckett characters just as it now tells the stories of a series of narrators, all of whom are composers of stories themselves, suggests the possibility that the one constant speaker behind all the characters, behind even the Unnamable, and embodied in a certain manner in each of them is the author, Samuel Beckett himself.[4] If this is the case, then Beckett has done in a twentieth-century context something similar to what Dante did in a fourteenth-century context : he has constructed a portrait of man by way of a portrait of the artist. It is significant that one of the most striking common features of the chararcters of the trilogy is something they do not share with most of mankind : they are all writers. Each is a compulsive writer and thinker. Thus each has a compulsion to consciousness and to reflection upon his own consciousness. If man as such is characterized by a compulsion to consciousness, then Beckett's characters can be considered representative of mankind in that they represent not the average man but man at his most conscious.

Both Beckett and Dante have been selective in their portraits of the artist, and both have selected those elements in their own experience that could be used most effectively and in the most representative manner for a portrait that would embody in a particular figure or group of figures the attitudes and concerns of an age. In the case of Dante it was an age in which man saw his entire human world and even the nonhuman cosmos as embraced within a single over-all vision of redemption through the cross of Christ. For Beckett and his age there is no redemption and the only cross is that upon which he himself is crucified, the almost unendurable burden of a consciousness absurdly divided against itself and condemned endlessly to seek meaning in a meaningless universe.

CHAPTER VI

Disillusionment with Knowledge and Action

Whether the principal characters of the trilogy are to be interpreted as merely various aspects or incarnations of a single personality or whether they are to be interpreted as distinct individuals, they definitely represent successive degrees of knowledge and experience. Taken as a series, they move from concern with externals to concern with the internal and from a belief in the possibility of knowledge to complete uncertainty. Moran represents the first stage in this process of growth. He associates his anxieties entirely with external sources and tends strongly to believe that if he could only understand and correct these external causes he might find relief from the anxiety itself. The process moves from these naïve illusions of Moran through a relatively more sophisticated state of illusion in Molloy and a relatively more advanced stage of disillusionment in Malone to the total, desperate disillusionment of the Unnamable. Basically there are three types of illusion that beset the characters of the trilogy—the illusion of the possibility of objective knowledge, the illusion of freedom or of motivated behavior, and the illusion that the principal causes of their anxiety are external rather than within themselves.

The story of Moran is the story of a complacently extroverted bourgeois, comfortably embedded in a world of possessions, confronted midway through his life with the insistent demands of an inner reality to be recognized and with a dawning realization that external possessions provide no genuine security. Moran's quest for Molloy is primarily Moran's gradual discovery of the Molloy within him, the assimilation of a bourgeois to a bum.

At the beginning of his story, Moran describes the fragile peace of 'that memorable August Sunday' on which his quest began :

> The weather was fine. I watched absently the coming and going of my bees. . . . All was still. Not a breath. From my neighbours' chimneys the smoke rose straight and blue. None but tranquil sounds, the clicking of mallet and ball, a rake on pebbles, a distant lawn-mower, the bell of my beloved church. And birds of course, blackbird and thrush, their song sadly dying, vanquished by the heat, and leaving dawn's high boughs for the bushes' gloom. Contentedly I inhaled the scent of my lemon-verbena.
>
> In such surroundings slipped away my last moments of peace and happiness [*Molloy*, pp. 126-27].

All this is shattered by the entry of Gaber, who brings word from 'the chief' that Moran is to find Molloy.

From the very beginning this quest takes on the form of a haunting, inward preoccupation that surprises Moran :

> That a man like me, so meticulous and calm in the main, so patiently turned towards the outer world as towards the lesser evil, creature of his house, of his garden, of his few poor possessions, discharging faithfully and ably a revolting function, reining back his thoughts within the limits of the calculable so great is his horror of fancy, that a man so contrived . . . should let himself be haunted and possessed by chimeras . . . [*Molloy* p. 156].

He is surprised that a person orderly and rationalistic in the externals of life should find within himself forces so disrupting and irrational : 'How little one is at one with oneself, good God. I who prided myself on being a sensible man, cold as crystal and as free from spurious depth' (p. 154).

The change Moran finds himself going through resembles that described by Carl Jung, the inventor of the concepts of extrovert and introvert, as inevitable to a person approaching the middle of life. According to Jung, a person reaching this point finds changes taking place within him which aim at correcting or compensating for an unbalance that has developed in one's psychology during the first half of one's life.[1] Thus a person like Moran, 'so meticulous and calm in the main, so patiently turned towards the

outer world as towards the lesser evil, creature of his house, of
his garden, of his few poor possessions,' would find himself becoming
fascinated by an inner reality of which he had never been aware
and which would take the form of an exact opposite of himself.

This is in fact exactly what Moran goes through. He finds
himself the theater of involuntary processes that are unexpected,
which he cannot understand, and which frighten him : 'For it is
no small matter, for a grown man thinking he is done with surprises,
to see himself the theatre of such ignominy. I had really good
cause to be alarmed' (p. 153). And when he discusses Molloy he
describes him as an inner upheaval : 'He had only to rise up within
me for me to be filled with panting' (p. 154). What Moran describes seems to be less the real Molloy than simply the opposite of
all that Moran thinks himself to be :

> He rolled his head, uttering incomprehensible words.
> He was massive and hulking, to the point of misshapenness.
> And, without being black, of a dark colour.
> He was forever on the move. I had never seen him rest.
> Occasionally he stopped and glared furiously about him.
> This was how he came to me, at long intervals. Then I was
> nothing but uproar, bulk, rage, suffocation, effort unceasing,
> frenzied and vain. Just the opposite of myself, in fact. It was a
> change [*Molloy*, p. 155].

It would be difficult to determine that Beckett was consciously
and deliberately using Jung's patterns of psychic development in
Moran, but the similarity is striking. It should also be noted that
although Moran's quest seems to involve an assimilation of Moran
to Molloy according to Moran's account of it, this may be merely
accidental, that is, Moran may only be projecting the pattern of
his inner transformation into the external quest. This may be the
reason for the obvious differences between the real Molloy with
which the reader is already familiar and Moran's inner Molloy
described above. But then, on the other hand, the real Molloy may
actually be representative of a stage of development that Moran
is able to apprehend only imperfectly and with only partial accuracy
as 'uproar, bulk, rage, suffocation, effort unceasing, frenzied and
vain.'

Whatever may be the answer to these questions, it is evident that for Moran the quest for Molloy is an inner adventure as well as an outer one. It is also rather frightening to him; he undertakes it with reluctance. When Gaber first appears to bring him his assignment, he tries to refuse it, and even after he accepts it he avoids facing its seriousness by giving his mind to all sorts of trivia :

> And tonight I find it strange I could have thought of such things, I mean my son, my lack of breeding, Father Ambrose, Verger Joly with his register, at such a time. Had I not something better to do, after what I had just heard? The fact is I had not yet begun to take the matter seriously. And I am all the more surprised as such light-mindedness was not like me. Or was it in order to win a few more moments of peace that I instinctively avoided giving my mind to it? [*Molloy*, p. 131].

But it is not something he can put off effectively by any deliberate effort, for it is a force that works in him independently of his will : '. . . the poison was already acting on me, the poison I had just been given. I stirred restlessly in my arm-chair. . . . The colour and weight of the world were changing already, soon I would have to admit I was anxious' (*Molloy*, pp. 131-32).

Although Moran feels that the quest is an important duty, he persistently attempts to avoid thinking about it. Even when he tries to give it his attention he continues partially to avoid it : 'My concern at first was only with its immediate vexations and the preparations they demanded of me. The kernel of the affair I continued to shirk (*Molloy*, p. 134).

One of the most important aspects of the quest is that it requires him to leave the comfortable little world of his possessions. This he finds difficult to do. Looking back on the beginning from the time of writing he remembers how he sought to take his possessions with him in the form of his autocycle and reflects on how contrary this was to what his task required of him :

> I liked leaving on my autocycle, I was partial to this way of getting about. And in my ignorance of the reasons against it I decided to leave on my autocycle. Thus was inscribed, on the threshold of the Molloy affair, the fatal pleasure principle [*Molloy*, pp. 134-35].

His reluctance to give up his bourgeois world seems to be the main thing that prevents him from engaging wholeheartedly in his task, but in reflecting on this he prefers to blame his property for holding him back rather than to recognize that the fault lies not in his possessions but in himself. It is evidence of the progress he has made that at the time of writing he can analyze this tendency to attribute his inner problems to external causes: 'I said, There is something in this house tying my hands. A man like me cannot forget, in his evasions, what it is he evades. I went down to the garden and moved about in the almost total darkness' (p. 167). Walking there, he thinks about various subjects besides his work, including his son, and he concludes his later account ironically with: 'What would I have done that day without my son to distract me? My duty perhaps' (p. 168). He realizes at the time of writing that it was by choice and with self-deception that he attributed his failure to his property:

> Finding my spirits as low in the garden as in the house, I turned to go in, saying to myself it was one of two things, either my house had nothing to do with the kind of nothingness in the midst of which I stumbled or else the whole of my little property was to blame. To adopt this latter hypothesis was to condone what I had done and, in advance, what I was to do, pending my departure. It brought me a semblance of pardon and a brief moment of factitious freedom. I therefore adopted it [*Molloy*, p. 168].

In thinking about leaving his house and possessions he experiences a certain inner conflict, since although he is reluctant to lose the life with which he is familiar, he feels fascinated by the call into the unknown. At times he appears to be feeling an eager anticipation for the new and an impatience with the old: 'And if I whistled fitfully while revolving these lugubrious thoughts, I suppose it was because I was happy at heart to leave my house, my garden, my village, I who usually left them with regret' (p. 171). This insouciance is belied, however, by the nostalgia with which he looks back longingly at his house and garden just as he is passing through the gate on his journey: 'And so I turned again a last time towards my little all, before I left it, in the hope of keeping it' (p. 175).

The same divided state of mind is seen in his reactions to the physical changes he goes through during the process of his assimilation to Molloy. Molloy, in his part of the book, was in an advanced stage of decrepitude. Moran, when he sets out on his quest, is still in fairly good physical condition. As he progresses, however, his legs gradually stiffen until movement, as it was for Molloy, becomes extremely laborious and painful. When he is struck one night during the journey by 'a fulgurating pain' which shoots through his knee, he tries to dismiss it with the thought, 'It's a touch of neuralgia' (p. 190), but wakes up the next morning unable to walk. Painful as 'this new cross' is to him he tries to conceal the affliction from his son. Thinking about the fact later, he wonders if perhaps he does not unconsciously desire his illness :

> I asked myself certain questions. Why had I not told my son to bring me back something for my leg? Why had I hidden my condition from him? Was I secretly glad that this had happened to me, perhaps even to the point of not wanting to get well? [*Molloy*, p. 199].

Even at the time of one of the more striking irruptions from within he still has a tendency to turn away to avoid thinking about it. That he begins the description of this event with the words, 'And on myself too I pored' (p. 203), is evidence of the persisting fascination his inner depths have for him, but when he describes the vision of a vague face floating up out of his depths, he also says that he gave it little attention and actually sought to divert his mind elsewhere :

> And then I saw a little globe swaying up slowly from the depths, through the quiet water, smooth at first . . . then little by little a face, with holes for the eyes and mouth and other wounds. . . . But I confess I attended but absently to these poor figures, in which I suppose my sense of disaster sought to contain itself. . . . And doubtless I should have gone from discovery to discovery, concerning myself, if I had persisted. But at the first faint light, I mean in these wild shadows gathering about me, dispensed by a vision or by an effort of thought, at the first light I fled to other cares. . . . Similarly the missing instructions concerning Molloy, when I felt them stirring in the depths of my memory, I turned from them in haste towards other unknowns [*Molloy*, p. 204].

Immediately after this episode an incident occurs that is of obscure import but which seems to represent the simultaneous attraction and repulsion Moran feels toward both his old self and the new inner reality that he is seeking. Moran is alone at night making a fire and is taken by surprise when a dim man 'dim of face and dim of body' comes up behind him. The dim man is dressed like a clown or bum, and in this he resembles Molloy : 'He was on the small side, but thick-set. He wore a thick navy-blue suit (double-breasted) of hideous cut and a pair of outrageously wide black shoes, with the toecaps higher than the uppers' (p. 206). But in his features he resembles Moran : 'But all this was nothing compared to the face which I regret to say vaguely resembled my own, less the refinement of course, same little abortive moustache, same little ferrety eyes, same paraphimosis of the nose, and a thin red mouth . . .' (p. 206). Although the exchange between them seems relatively innocuous as recounted, for some reason the man frightens Moran, who, apparently in the grip of an irresistible terror, kills him :

> He thrust his hand at me. I have an idea I told him once again to get out of my way. I can still see the hand coming towards me, pallid, opening and closing. As if self-propelled. I do not know what happened then. But a little later, perhaps a long time later, I found him stretched on the ground his head in a pulp [*Molloy*, p. 207].

Apparently the man represents for Moran the changes that are taking place within him, which in this instance he tries to evade by the destruction of that which symbolizes them. When he sub- sequently crawls around searching for his keys, which had come loose from his keychain, he seems to be attempting to reconsolidate his hold on his bourgeois identity. Earlier he had given an account of these keys and chain which showed their great importance to him :

> I have a huge bunch of keys, it weighs over a pound. Not a door, not a drawer in my house but the key to it goes with me, wherever I go. I carry them in the right-hand pocket of my trousers, of my breeches in this case. A massive chain, attached to my braces, prevents me from losing them [*Molloy*, p. 172].

In that passage the keys seemed to represent to him his house and possessions, and now it would seem to be these he is trying to recover as he gathers up his scattered keys, though the weakening of his grip on the old Moran is seen in his inability to find all of them : '. . . finding no more keys, I said, There is no use my counting them, for I do not know how many there were. And my eyes resumed their search. But finally I said, Hell to it, I'll do with those I have' (p. 209).

His hat, which he has also lost in the scuffle with the dim man, seems to be another symbol to him of his bourgeois life. When he was setting out on the quest, he carefully made an elastic chin strap for his old straw boater so that it would be sure to stay on. Now as he gropes around for it, he seems to be trying to recover his old self. Again, though, it is an imperfect recovery since the hat has suffered damage : '. . . one of the holes from the elastic had expanded to the edge of the rim and consequently was no longer a hole, but a slit' (p. 209).

As he proceeds on his journey he has a definite sense that he has changed and is still changing. He also feels that the change is somehow beyond his comprehension (p. 211):

> *Question.* How did I feel?
> *Answer.* Much as usual.
> *Question.* And yet I had changed and was still changing?
> *Answer.* Yes.
> *Question.* And in spite of this I felt much as usual?
> *Answer.* Yes.
> *Question.* How was this to be explained?
> *Answer.*

That the change is an assimilation to Molloy is not evident to Moran since he knows relatively little of the real Molloy, but it is evident to the reader who knows already that, for example, Molloy had one bad leg as Moran now has. The reader, remembering Molloy's description of how he pedaled his bicycle with one leg, can appreciate the dramatic irony in Moran's saying :

> I had told him [his son] to keep an eye out, on his expeditions, for a second bicycle, light and inexpensive. For I was weary of the carrier and I also saw the day approaching when my son would no longer have the strength to pedal for the two of us. And I believed I was capable, more than that, I knew I was capable with a little practice, of learning to pedal with one leg [*Molloy*, pp. 220-21].

This process of transformation into a person like Molloy is not finished by the end of the book, but apparently it has advanced far enough by page 223 for Youdi to be satisfied that Moran has found Molloy, since Gaber comes and tells him he is to return home. The continuation of the process can be seen during the journey home in the physical changes that take place in him. At first he just becomes increasingly strange to himself : 'Physically speaking it seemed to me I was now becoming rapidly unrecognizable. And when I passed my hands over my face . . . the face my hands felt was not my face any more, and the hands my face felt were my hands no longer' (p. 233). But as he proceeds, it is clear to the reader that Moran is being transformed into a bum, like Molloy :

> . . . I had to part with my straw, not made to resist the rigours of winter, and with my stockings (two pairs) which the cold and damp, the trudging and the lack of laundering facilities had literally annihilated. But I let out my braces to their fullest extent and my knickerbockers, very baggy as the fashion is, came down to my calves [*Molloy*, pp. 233-34].

Through all of this Moran retains the divided state of mind the reader has already seen. Even dressed as shabbily as any bum, he clings to the last traces of bourgeois respectability represented by his necktie : 'My hard collars, yes, I discarded them all, and even before they were quite worn and torn. But I kept my tie, I even wore it, knotted round my bare neck, out of sheer bravado I suppose' (p. 234).

At the very end of his narrative he says, 'I am clearing out. Perhaps I shall meet Molloy,' and he professes detachment from his possessions : 'The house was empty. The company had cut off the light. They have offered to let me have it back. But I told them they could keep it. That is the kind of man I have become' (p. 240). He overestimates the change in himself, however. Unless he has changed rather suddenly from the type of person he was while writing his account, he still is not entirely detached from his possessions. On page 181, for example, he reveals, at the time of writing, a genuine terror at the idea of being divested of their support :

> It also tells me, this voice I am only just beginning to know,

that the memory of this work brought scrupulously to a close will help me to endure the long anguish of vagrancy and freedom. Does this mean I shall one day be banished from my house, from my garden, lose my trees, my lawns, my birds of which the least is known to me and the way all its own it has of singing, of flying, of coming up to me or fleeing at my coming, lose and be banished from the absurd comforts of my home where all is snug and neat and all those things at hand without which I could not bear being a man, where my enemies cannot reach me, which it was my life's work to build, to adorn, to perfect, to keep? I am too old to lose all this, and begin again, I am too old!

In another place he shows the same type of attachment to property in speaking of his grave : 'Some twenty paces from my wicket-gate the lane skirts the graveyard wall. . . . It is there I have my plot in perpetuity. As long as the earth endures that spot is mine, in theory' (pp. 184-85).

A more subtle way of externalizing his anxieties than by seeking a false security in possessions can be seen during most of his story in Moran's attitude toward his religion and toward his employer and in the manner in which he tends to associate the two in his thinking. His religion tends to seem magical to him, and he thinks of it primarily as an external system of authority. The organization he works for, on the other hand, takes on quasi-religious connotations in his mind. Since Moran is the narrator of his own story, there is no way of knowing what type of person Youdi might be if seen through the eyes of another observer, but for Moran he seems, like Watt's Mr Knott, to have the type of power, authority, and omniscience that one would usually attribute only to God.[2]

The magical character of Moran's religion becomes evident when he wonders why the Communion he has received is producing no visible effect :

The host, it is only fair to say, was lying heavy on my stomach. And as I made my way home I felt like one who, having swallowed a pain-killer, is first astonished, then indignant, on obtaining no relief. And I was almost ready to suspect Father Ambrose, alive to my excesses of the forenoon, of having fobbed me off with unconsecrated bread. Or of mental reservation as

D

he pronounced the magic words [*Molloy*, p. 139].

Moran thinks of Communion only as a sort of tonic, 'To buck me up' (p. 129), and has no conception of grace as involving an invisible, moral influence rather than a tangible physical or emotional effect. He wonders on page 132 if the Eucharist can 'produce the same effect, taken on top of beer, however light' and reflects 'But God would know, sooner or later.' This shows that his idea of God is more like that of the remote head of some secular system of authority than like the omnipresent and omniscient God of Christianity.

That Youdi, his 'chief,' is cloaked in a numinous and quasi-religious authority for Moran can be seen in many references to him that sound more like references to the Old Testament God. For example, when his son becomes ill, he is afraid he might be struck by lightning if, by postponing his departure until his son is better, he fails to keep the letter of Youdi's commandments :

> Was not this the providential hindrance for which I could not be held responsible? Doubtless, but I would never dare invoke it. I was not going to expose myself to thunderbolts which might be fatal, simply because my son had the gripes. . . . It was not for nothing I had studied the old testament [*Molloy*, p. 162].

And when he says on page 147,

> . . . this lucidity was so acute at times that I came even to doubt the existence of Gaber himself. And if I had not hastily sunk back into my darkness I might have gone to the extreme of conjuring away the chief too and regarding myself as solely responsible for my wretched existence,

he sounds like an incipient atheist daring to doubt the existence of God.

In one place he even seems to attribute to Youdi the omniscience with which he failed to credit the God of his formal religion. When Moran speculates about Molloy on page 157 he decides that there must be four Molloys, 'he that inhabited me, my caricature of same, Gaber's and the man of flesh and blood somewhere awaiting me.' Then he goes on to add a fifth Molloy, that of Youdi, saying, however, 'But would not this fifth Molloy necessarily coincide with the fourth, the real one as the saying is, him dogged by his shadow?' This sounds rather like the sort of comment a medieval theologian might have made speaking of God's perfect and immediate knowledge of creatures.

When he goes on to say, 'And let us not meddle either with the question as to how far these five Molloys were constant and how far subject to variation. For there was this about Youdi, that he changed his mind with great facility' (pp. 157-58), he seems to be attributing creative power to Youdi's knowledge, again likening him to God or, more accurately, assimilating his idea of Youdi to his idea of the divine. If this is the case, then the idea of a changing God places contingency and uncertainty at the centre of Moran's universe instead of the Absolute that God is usually supposed to represent.

All of Moran's statements about Youdi actually tell the reader more about Moran than they do about Youdi. As much as Youdi resembles God, there is no reason to suppose that Youdi simply is God; what is important is that, whatever Youdi may be in reality, he looks like God to Moran, who is continually looking for something outside himself, both in religion and in the organization he works for upon which to unload the responsibility for his life. Another instance of the same tendency is seen in Moran's reaction to a shepherd he meets as he enters the region of Ballyba. Moran and his son are riding along on their bicycle when Moran catches sight of a shepherd and tells his son to stop. The episode is marked by an air of great solemnity: 'The silence was absolute. Profound in any case. All things considered it was a solemn moment' (p. 217). The shepherd makes a tremendous impression on Moran: 'How I would love to dwell upon him. His dog loved him, his sheep did not fear him. . . . I longed to say, Take me with you, I will serve you faithfully, just for a place to lie and a little food' (pp. 217-18). Here again Moran's desire to relieve himself of the burden of his responsibilities makes of an otherwise ordinary person a figure of religious stature—one of the traditional titles of Christ is the Good Shepherd.

The most important change that takes place in Moran during his quest is the shift of his attention, even though involuntary, from these various systems of external authority to the internal authority of the voice. The change is gradual. It is foreshadowed

early in the story by Moran's failure to find guidance in God—
'Alone, my hands clasped until it seemed my knuckles would crack,
I asked the Lord for guidance. Without result' (p. 137)—but it
is not until much later, after he has been ordered home by Youdi,
that he hears the voice for the first time, and then it means little
to him : 'I have spoken of a voice giving me orders, or rather
advice. It was on the way home I heard it for the first time. I
paid no attention to it' (p. 233).

By the time of writing, however, the voice is really in control
of him, completely replacing the authority of Youdi :

> . . . the voice I listen to needs no Gaber to make it heard. For
> it is within me and exhorts me to continue to the end the faithful
> servant I have always been, of a cause that is not mine. . . .
> And this with hatred in my heart, and scorn, of my master
> and his designs [*Molloy*, p. 180].

It is still difficult for him to see a rational guide in the voice, but
he chooses to follow it in preference to any external authority :

> Yes, it is rather an ambiguous voice and not always easy to
> follow, in its reasonings and decrees. But I follow it none the
> less, more or less. . . . And I feel I shall follow it from this day
> forth, no matter what it commands. And when it ceases, leaving
> me in doubt and darkness, I shall wait for it to come back, and
> do nothing, even though the whole world, through the channel
> of its innumerable authorities speaking with one accord, should
> enjoin upon me this and that, under pain of unspeakable punish-
> ments [*Molloy*, pp. 180-81].

This shift in Moran's allegiance from the external authority of
Youdi to the internal authority of the voice is obviously an important part of the process of growth Moran is going through, but
the exact meaning of the shift is not easy to define. Youdi, as he is
presented to us, is a mysterious figure. Moran sees him as the
principal immediate representative in his life of external authority,
but one wonders why a simply external authority would be so
interested in sending Moran on a quest the goal of which seems
to be that he is to become assimilated to the person he is pursuing.
If Youdi represents in the book, as he well may, just one external
embodiment of a general force in the nature of things that leads

one to become more aware of one's inner reality, then the change taking place in Moran is not so much a change of allegiance as a change simply in Moran's way of perceiving the forces that drive him. This, of course, would be an important step toward understanding the true nature of these forces.

During the course of his narrative, Moran makes comments from time to time that show how little regard he has at present for all the former sources of authority in his life. On page 144, for example, he says God is beginning to disgust him, and in another place he says, 'There are men and there are things, to hell with animals. And with God' (p. 227). On page 222, expressing his contempt for Youdi, he also mentions an Obidil—whose name is libido spelled more or less backward—apparently another deity to collapse :

> And with regard to the Obidil, of whom I have refrained from speaking, until now, and whom I so longed to see face to face, all I can say with regard to him is this, that I never saw him, either face to face or darkly, perhaps there is no such person, that would not greatly surprise me. And at the thought of the punishments Youdi might inflict upon me I was seized by such a mighty fit of laughter that I shook. . . .

The 'either face to face or darkly' with reference to Obidil makes him another God-figure by allusion to the famous passage of St Paul in I Corinthians 13.[3]

That religion is still important to him on his way home can be seen from the fact that he finds himself preoccupied with theological questions, but even some of these indicate a growing disillusionment with the God of formal religion :

13. What was God doing with himself before the creation? [More vulgarly in the French text, p. 259, '*Que foutait Dieu avant la création?*']
14. Might not the beatific vision become a source of boredom, in the long run? [*Molloy*, p. 229].

Shortly after this, thinking about the mysterious dance of his bees, he says, 'And I would never do my bees the wrong I had done my God, to whom I had been taught to ascribe my angers, fears, desires, and even my body' (p. 233). The same disillusionment with

the Christianity he had been taught in childhood can be seen in
a more advanced stage in one of the last statements he makes at
the end of his account :

> I have spoken of a voice telling me things. I was getting to know
> it better now, to understand what it wanted. It did not use the
> words that Moran had been taught when he was little and that
> he in his turn had taught to his little one. So that at first I
> did not know what it wanted. But in the end I understood this
> language [*Molloy*, p. 241].

Before setting out to continue his quest, now under the direction
of the voice, he indicates that he is abandoning formal religion :

> One day I received a visit from Father Ambrose. Is it possible !
> he said when he saw me. I think he really liked me, in his own
> way. I told him not to count on me any more. He began to talk.
> He was right. Who is not right? I left him. I am clearing out.
> Perhaps I shall meet Molloy. My knee is no better. It is no
> worse either. I have crutches now. I shall go faster, all will go
> faster. They will be happy days. I shall learn [*Molloy*, p. 240].

Molloy is considerably further along the path of experience than
Moran. He has already passed through a disillusionment with
most of the systems of knowledge with which man tries to bring
order into life :

> Yes, I once took an interest in astronomy, I don't deny it.
> Then it was geology that killed a few years for me. The next pain
> in the balls was anthropology and the other disciplines, such as
> psychiatry, that are connected with it, disconnected, then con-
> nected again, according to the latest discoveries. What I liked
> in anthropology was its inexhaustible faculty of negation, its
> relentless definition of man, as though he were no better than
> God, in terms of what he is not, [*sic*] But my ideas on this
> subject were always horribly confused, for my knowledge of men
> was scant and the meaning of being beyond me. Oh I've tried
> everything. In the end it was magic that had the honour of
> my ruins, and still today, when I walk there, I find its vestiges
> [*Molloy*, p. 52].

One of these vestiges of magic can be seen in his later speculation that when he tried to leave Lousse's house she may have tried to hold him back 'by spells' (p. 79). To replace science with magic is in effect to say that all human attempts at knowledge culminate in the recognition of the ultimate mysteriousness of reality.

The kind of psychiatry he was once interested in must have been Freudian, since there seem to be traces of a kind of vague Freudianism in his thinking. Speaking of his mother's attempts to abort him before his birth, he says : 'And if ever I'm reduced to looking for a meaning to my life, you never can tell, it's in that old mess I'll stick my nose to begin with, the mess of that poor old uniparous whore and myself . . .' (*Molloy*, p. 23). This would seem a Freudian approach to the quest for understanding of one's life. Another apparent vestige of Freudianism can be found on page 78 in Molloy's reference to the repression of an unpleasant memory. Talking about an old woman with whom he once used to make love, or something like it, he speculates on the possibility that she was actually a man and adds that if she were and it had been discovered after her death 'it is quite possible that the fact of having found a man when they should have found a woman was immediately repressed and forgotten, by the few unfortunate enough to know about it.' Molloy could hardly take his Freudianism very seriously in the present, however, since he now speaks of it and all other intellectual disciplines that try to make sense of the mysteries of man as a 'pain in the balls.'

At present he is much more interested in things than in theories : '. . . to restore silence is the role of objects' (p. 16). He has a number of possessions to which he is very attached : his sucking stones, for example, his rusty fruit-knife, his hat. On several different occasions he speaks of the necessity of eventually drawing up an inventory of them. Molloy's attachment to objects differs from Moran's, however, in that it does not seem to involve a theory of property rights. It apparently gave Moran a feeling of stability to be able to say something like 'As long as the earth endures that spot is mine, in theory' (pp. 184-85). Molloy tends to look upon his possessions simply as things he has picked up here and there, and he seems to use them more as playthings than as real bulwarks against insecurity.

It is probably significant that the object to which Molloy seems most attached is a small silver knife-rest that he stole from Lousse. He does not himself realize that it is a knife-rest. In fact he has no idea what it is, and this is the reason it fascinates him :

> This strange instrument I think I still have somewhere, for I could never bring myself to sell it, even in my worst need, for I could never understand what possible purpose it could serve, nor even contrive the faintest hypothesis on the subject. And from time to time I took it from my pocket and gazed upon it, with an astonished and affectionate gaze . . . [*Molloy*, p. 85].

One of Molloy's more troublesome problems is that he is a compulsive thinker with no confidence in knowledge. His disillusionment with the various learned disciplines he had studied has not delivered him from the need to go on thinking about the world around him and trying to discover a meaningful pattern in it. It is as though there were a thinking reflex that continues to operate by itself after one has become consciously disillusioned with reason. When a shepherd and his flock pass by at the beginning of the book (p. 38), Molloy wonders long afterward where they were going and what became of them, and when he wakes up in the night at Lousse's house and sees the moon through the window, he can not help wondering whether 'the moon was moving from left to right, or the room was moving from right to left, or both together perhaps, or both were moving from left to right, but the room not so fast as the moon, or from right to left, but the moon not so fast as the room' (p. 51).

The value of an object like the knife-rest for Molloy is that being a complete mystery it is something he knows in advance to be unintelligible. Since his mind is compelled to think, he can let it think endlessly about the knife-rest with no danger of falling into the illusion that meaning could ever be found in it :

> . . . for a certain time I think it inspired me with a kind of veneration, for there was no doubt in my mind that it was not an object of virtu, but that it had a most specific function always to be hidden from me. I could therefore puzzle over it endlessly without the least risk. For to know nothing is nothing, not to want to know anything likewise, but to be beyond knowing anything, to know you are beyond knowing anything, that is when peace enters in, to the soul of the incurious seeker. It is then the true division begins of twenty-two by seven for example,

and the pages fill with the true ciphers at last [*Molloy*, pp. 85-86].

Twenty-two divided by seven equals $3.142857142857 \ldots$, a calculation that can be continued endlessly.[4]

Puzzles are not always pleasurable to Molloy, however. This can be seen in the episode of the sucking-stones. What goes wrong here is that although he solves the problem of how to carry the stones in his four pockets in such a way that he sucks each of them in succession, his solution lacks symmetry. The distress he feels at this can be clearly seen in the tone with which he describes the solution :

> But I was tired, but I was tired, and I contented myself in-gloriously with the first solution that was a solution, to this problem. But not to go over the heartbreaking stages through which I passed before I came to it, here it is, in all its hideous-ness. All (all!) that was necessary was to put for example, to begin with, six stones in the right pocket of my greatcoat, or supply-pocket, five in the right pocket of my trousers . . . [*Molloy*, p. 96].

and so on. It is as if symmetry replaces meaning for Molloy as the goal of thought.[5] In one place he even says that he has 'a mania for symmetry' (p. 114).

Although Molloy finds a certain amount of solace in mysteries and in symmetry he is aware that these are only human distractions in an empty and meaningless universe. Sometimes the realization of this comes to him and sometimes it does not; it is not something that he controls :

> And the thing in ruins. I don't know what it is, what it was, nor whether it is not less a question of ruins than the indestruc-tible chaos of timeless things . . . it is not the kind of place where you go, but where you find yourself, sometimes, not knowing how, and which you cannot leave at will, and where you find yourself without any pleasure, but with more perhaps than in those places you can escape from, by making an effort, places full of mystery, full of the familiar mysteries [*Molloy*, pp. 52-53].

Moran is a person who has not yet reached this vision, but he

also goes through a process of disillusionment with knowledge, and
in his case also a mystery seems to provide the most satisfactory
relief from a compulsion to understand. At the time of writing
he has progressed considerably from the type of person he was
at the beginning of his journey. In describing how he felt about
the changes taking place within him before he set out he says,
'I could not understand what was happening to me. I found it
painful at that period not to understand' (p. 139). At the time
of writing he probably still feels some discomfort at not understanding things, but he also feels a deep distrust of the very
possibility of knowledge :

> What I assert, deny, question, in the present, I still can. But
> mostly I shall use the various tenses of the past. For mostly I
> do not know, it is perhaps no longer so, it is too soon to know,
> I simply do not know, perhaps shall never know [*Molloy*,
> pp. 143-44].

After he has already advanced some distance in the process of
disillusionment with knowledge he comes to find relief from thought
in the contemplation of the mysterious and unfathomable dance
of his bees. While at home he had spent many hours watching the
figures and rhythms of the dances done by the bees returning to
the hive laden with nectar. He had previously devised theories
as to the possible meaning of the dances, but their real fascination
for him now lies in the impossibility of ever definitely assigning
any meaning to them :

> And in spite of all the pains I had lavished on these problems,
> I was more than ever stupefied by the complexity of this in-
> numerable dance, involving doubtless other determinants of
> which I had not the slightest idea. And I said, with rapture,
> Here is something I can study all my life, and never under-
> stand [*Molloy*, p. 232].

Malone, in his volume, has progressed further in the process of
disillusionment than has either Moran or Molloy. He is disillusioned
with knowledge, of course, but he also has less confidence in the
power of devices such as mysteries to give him real relief from
compulsive cogitation. When Malone mentions a mystery at one
point, his mystery sounds like a parody of Molloy's knife-rest

rather than a device that Malone takes seriously. Malone's mystery is just a package, and its mysteriousness is given to it arbitrarily by Malone simply by his decision not to unwrap it, nor does he suggest that it could deliver him even momentarily from his compulsive mental activity: 'I also discovered a little packet tied up in age-yellowed newspaper. . . . I resolved, I don't know why, not to undo it. . . . It will be my little mystery, all my own' (*Malone,* p. 21).

At the very beginning of his narrative Malone expresses a desire to be free from the necessity of thinking ceaselessly: 'I shall not answer any more questions. I shall even try not to ask myself any more' (p. 2). But within only a few pages his anguished tone betrays the intense despair of his realization that no such release is possible: 'Somewhere in this turmoil thought struggles on, it too wide of the mark. It too seeks me, as it always has, where I am not to be found. It too cannot be quiet. On others let it wreak its dying rage, and leave me in peace' (*Malone,* p. 9). So he continues, in spite of his intentions, to pose questions and to grope after answers.

His present reflections on a memory from his childhood show his current disillusionment with knowledge:

One day we [Malone and his mother] were walking along the road. . . . I said, The sky is further away than you think, is it not, mama? It was without malice, I was simply thinking of all the leagues that separated me from it. She replied, to me her son, It is precisely as far away as it appears to be. She was right [*Malone,* p. 98].

But this conscious realization that it is less unreasonable to accept appearances at face value than to attempt to know the realities that are supposed to lie behind them does not free him from the necessity to go on, over and over, trying to know with a knowledge that is empty and absurd.

Malone also gives evidence of a greater realization than had either Moran or Molloy that to attribute one's anxiety to external causes is to cultivate an illusion. He comments ironically on the need Macmann and others feel to attribute their dissatisfaction with life to external causes:

For people are never content to suffer, but they must have heat
and cold, rain and its contrary which is fine weather, and with
that love, friendship, black skin and sexual and peptic deficiency
for example, in short the furies and frenzies happily too numerous
to be numbered of the body including the skull and its annexes,
whatever that means, such as the clubfoot, in order that they
may know very precisely what exactly it is that dares prevent
their happiness from being unalloyed [*Malone*, p. 70].

But again, his conscious realization of this psychological mechanism
does not deliver him from the irrational compulsion continually
to seek comfort in external sources, such as his possessions, or to
attribute his troubles to the agency of forces collectively described
as 'the powers that be' or simply as 'they,' who he believes have
always been hostile to him (see p. 5, for example).

Again and again, throughout his account, he mentions his
possessions and the need he feels to make an inventory of them.
In one place (p. 20) he even adds, 'I presume it is an obsession,'
in reference to this intention of making an inventory. In another
place he speculates that his possessions may deserve the credit for
having protected him from even more futile forms of escape from
anxiety :

And but for the company of these little objects which I picked
up here and there, when out walking, and which sometimes
gave me the impression that they too needed me, I might have
been reduced to the society of nice people or to the consolations
of some religion or other . . . [*Malone*, p. 75].

Nevertheless, a few pages later his attachment to his possessions
displays a childishness and irrationality apparent even to him :

Perhaps I should call in all my possessions such as they are and
take them into bed with me. Would that be any use? I suppose
not. But I may. I have always that resource. When it is light
enough to see. Then I shall have them all round me, on top
of me, under me, in the corner there will be nothing left, all
will be in the bed, with me [*Malone*, p. 79].

The Unnamable represents the type of person Malone would be
if deprived of all external distractions and the comfort of his

possessions. At the very beginning he expresses his intention to pass the time telling stories, but he seems a little bewildered without the presence of things :

> I shall not be alone in the beginning. I am of course alone. Alone. That is soon said. Things have to be soon said. And how can one be sure in such darkness? I shall have company. In the beginning. A few puppets. Then I'll scatter them to the winds, if I can. And things, what is the correct attitude to adopt towards things? And, to begin with, are they necessary? What a question. But I have few illusions, things are to be expected. The best is not to decide anything, in this connexion, in advance. If a thing turns up, for some reason or another, take it into consideration [*Unnamable*, p. 4].

But things never do turn up, for any reason. All he has left is his stories, and the only illusion of which he has to be divested is the illusion that his characters are his puppets rather than he theirs.

It is the ultimate in irony that a series of characters or incarnations have to go through a process of disillusionment with the idea that the misery of their lives is due to external causes only to discover that the internal causes are also external in the sense that the characters have no control over them. Although the Unnamable starts off with the idea that he will tell stories to amuse himself, the horrifying truth gradually dawns on him that he is not telling them voluntarily. Nor can he even feel confident that it is he who is telling them rather than they who are telling him. By the end of his volume he realizes that the only certainty is the compulsion of a mental activity to keep going endlessly with no goal.

The realization of the compulsive character of his thought begins to enter his mind within a few pages when he finds himself preoccupied with questions : 'But the mere fact of asking myself such a question gives me to reflect. . . . Can it be I am the prey of a genuine preoccupation, of a need to know as one might say?' (p. 8). And two pages later he reveals increasing uneasiness about this tendency : 'Deplorable mania, when something happens, to inquire what' (p. 10).

When he first begins to realize that the process of thought in him is something outside his control he expresses the feeling that it is alien by attributing it to the voice of Mahood speaking within him :

It was he told me stories about me, lived in my stead, issued forth from me, came back to me, entered back into me, heaped stories on my head. I don't know how it was done. I always liked not knowing, but Mahood said it wasn't right. He didn't know either, but it worried him. It is his voice which has often, always, mingled with mine, and sometimes drowned it completely [*Unnamable*, p. 29].

The attempt to explain the problem through the hypothesis of another personality operating in him only leads him to greater confusion and to a complete disgust with the necessity to understand things that are unintelligible, including the identity of this other personality :

That the impossible should be asked of me, good, what else could be asked of me? But the absurd! Of me whom they have reduced to reason. It is true poor Worm is not to blame for this. That's soon said. But let me complete my views, before I shit on them. For if I am Mahood, I am Worm too, plop. Or if I am not yet Worm, I shall be when I cease to be Mahood, plop [*Unnamable*, p. 70].

By the end he has left such attempts at explanation behind. All that remains is his realization of the persistent presence of the voice speaking in and through him, which is independent of his volition and yet which he cannot wholly distinguish from himself :

. . . a voice like this, who can check it, it tries everything, it's blind, it seeks me blindly, in the dark, it seeks a mouth, to enter into . . . I don't know, I look too often as if I knew, it's the voice does that, it goes all knowing, to make me think I know, to make me think it's mine . . . [*Unnamable*, p. 174].

All it is is a meaningless process of consciousness that goes on and on under a compulsion to know, long after the goal of knowledge has been given up as illusory.

In *The Unnamable* the realization that mental activity is compulsive rather than motivated involves a disillusionment with the whole idea of free and motivated behavior. In the other characters of the trilogy this realization and this disillusionment are only budding, but as the characters progress in experience their disillusionment with knowledge is paralleled by a growing realization that freedom and motivation are also illusions.

On the last page of his account, Moran says about the voice he is now following, 'It told me to write the report. Does this mean I am freer now than I was?' (*Molloy*, p. 241). Moran is only beginning to wonder about the question of freedom. Molloy, however, is at a more advanced stage of disillusionment, and he has radical doubts as to the very existence of freedom. He is beginning to realize that he is driven by forces within, which he calls his 'imperatives' and which negate his freedom : 'But I could not stay in the forest I mean, I was not free to. . . . I would have had the feeling, if I had stayed in the forest, of going against an imperative, at least I had that impression' (*Molloy*, p. 116). Molloy still tries to understand these imperatives as free in the sense that they are motivated—he says they 'nearly all bore on the same question, that of my relations with my mother' (p. 117)—but he also casts doubt, at the time of writing, on the idea of motivation as such, describing motivated behavior as a kind of superstitious magic similar to the invocation of saints :

> My reasons? I had forgotten them. But I knew them, I must have known them, I had only to find them again and I would sweep, with the clipped wings of necessity, to my mother. Yes, it's all easy when you know why, a mere matter of magic. Yes, the whole thing is to know what saint to implore, any fool can implore him [*Molloy*, p. 35].

He is still using this magic, though half-believing in its efficacy, when the reader last sees him laboriously crawling through the forest : 'I was on my way to mother. And from time to time I said, Mother, to encourage me I suppose' (p. 122).

Malone's disillusionment with freedom is similarly incomplete. He touches on the subject in one place when he describes a world of people leaving their jobs in the evening and hurrying to various rendezvous or other distractions : 'And each one has his reasons, while wondering from time to time what they are worth, and if they are the true ones, for going where he is going rather than somewhere else, and the horse hardly less darkly than the men . . .' (*Malone*, p. 58). Somewhat later he begins to wonder about himself, whether the story-telling he likes to think he does by choice to

pass the time is not in fact a compulsion : 'I wonder if I shall
ever be able to stop. Perhaps I should throw away my lead' (p. 82).

It is only in the Unnamable, however, that the full, hopeless
realization of the compulsive character of human activity becomes
conscious, and it is he who first uses the word 'compulsion' to
describe it : '. . . the compulsion I am under to speak of them,
and therefore perhaps think of them a little (*Unnamable*, p. 18).
Speaking in the person of Mahood, the one-legged traveler, the
Unnamable completely rejects the idea that his activity has any
motivation at all : 'I had no wish to arrive, but I had to do my
utmost, in order to arrive. A desirable goal, no, I never had time
to dwell on that. To go on, I still call that on, to go on and get
on has been my only care . . .' (*Unnamable*, p. 45). Molloy,
referring to a passage from Geulincx's *Ethics*, had spoken of a
limited degree of freedom left to him by the 'imperatives' that
were driving him onward : 'I who had loved the image of old
Geulincx . . . who left me free, on the black boat of Ulysses, to
crawl towards the East along the deck. That is a great measure
of freedom for him who has not the pioneering spirit' (*Molloy*,
p. 68).[6] The Unnamable recalls this idea of freedom within compulsion, but he speaks of it as just one more of the illusions he
will have to outgrow :

I. Who might that be? The galley-man, bound for the Pillars
of Hercules, who drops his sweep under cover of night and
crawls between the thwarts, towards the rising sun, unseen by
the guard, praying for storm. Except that I've stopped praying
for anything. No, no, I'm still a suppliant. I'll get over it. . . .
It's like the other madness, the mad wish to know . . . [*Unnamable*, p. 68].

By the end of his volume he sees himself lost in a stream of thought
which, whether it is his in some sense or whether it is that of an
alien voice seeking him 'blindly in the dark,' is not something
he chooses but which, traveling nowhere, carries him along : '. . .
you don't try any more, no need to try, it goes on by itself, it
drags on by itself, from word to word, a labouring whirl, you
are in it somewhere, everywhere . . .' (*Unnamable*, p. 161).

CHAPTER VII

Longing for Silence

With their gradual realization that life is an endless and purposeless process of thinking, the characters of the trilogy come to long for silence or for death as a means to silence. As we have seen, it is only slowly that a full realization of the compulsive, involuntary nature of their consciousness grows in them. Their attitudes toward consciousness and toward death go through corresponding transformations. Moran, Molloy, and Malone long for death and silence, but they also dread them; it is only for the Unnamable, who seems to have already passed through the experience of physical death and found it an illusory hope that the longing for silence, the death of consciousness, becomes unequivocal.

Moran is still relatively naïve as compared with the others, and consequently he tends to feel more burdened by the need to keep moving physically than by the need to keep thinking. His distrust of consciousness is to a large extent revealed indirectly through, for example, the imagery he uses, especially imagery of light and darkness,[1] and it is not always easy to distinguish between an incipient desire for escape from consciousness as such and a mere reluctance to face the new experiences, the new life of the Molloy within, that he is called to endure. This ambiguity in Moran's thinking can be seen clearly in a passage relating to the discovery of his inner Molloy. Describing what he sees when looking within, he says, 'it was like a kind of clawing towards a light and countenance I could not name, that I had once known and long denied' (*Molloy*, p. 203). And at the end of the passage he says he would have learned more from this introspection if he had persisted :

'But at the first faint light, I mean in these wild shadows gathering about me, dispensed by a vision or by an effort of thought, at the first faint light I fled to other cares' (p. 204). Although light definitely stands for consciousness here, it is hard to tell whether the fear Moran feels of this light is revulsion toward consciousness as such or only fear of self-knowledge. On the other hand, however, when he describes history on page 178 as the 'exploits of the human race, in its slow ascension towards the light,' he is using light unequivocally to stand for consciousness in general, not only for consciousness of a particular matter, and when he expresses his horror at the return of light in the morning by saying, 'The sky was that horrible colour which heralds dawn' (p. 191), his aversion to light betrays a dislike of consciousness as such.

It must not be thought, though, that Moran uses light imagery only negatively or that his attitude toward consciousness is only one of aversion. He fears darkness just as much as light : he says that he will always follow the voice, a form of consciousness, and that 'when it ceases, leaving me in doubt and darkness, I shall wait for it to come back' (p. 181).

Molloy also uses light imagery, and with a similar ambiguity. When he first mentions light it is to call it a type of poison : '. . . the sun, hoisting itself higher and higher in the east, had poisoned me, while I slept' (p. 24). And when he dreams of peace and rest in some place of refuge within, he thinks of it as a place in which he will be free from such poisons : 'Yes, I was straining towards those spurious deeps, their lying promise of gravity and peace, from all my old poisons I struggled towards them, safely bound' (p. 27).

A more explicit equation of light with consciousness is found on page 42 in Molloy's reference to 'my insane demands for more light.' In the English translation the meaning of this statement is not completely clear, since it could refer simply to physical light, but that what is meant is the light of consciousness can be seen from the wording in the French text (p. 47) : *'mes folles prétentions de tirer quelque chose au clair'* '. . . to bring something to light'. Another explicit equation of light with consciousness occurs on page 117 :

It is true they [his 'imperatives'] nearly all bore on the same question, that of my relations with my mother, and on the importance of bringing as soon as possible some light to bear on these and even on the kind of light that should be brought to bear and the most effective means of doing so.

As his journey proceeds and his disillusionment with knowledge becomes more of a disgust with thought and the waking life in general, his simultaneous attraction to and repulsion from physical light parallels his divided state of mind toward consciousness as such. This complex attitude can be seen in, for example, his description of his feelings during his time in the forest :

> . . . though it is no part of my tottering intentions to treat here in full . . . these brief moments of the immemorial expiation, I shall nevertheless deal with them briefly . . . so that my story, so clear till now, may not end in darkness, the darkness of these towering forests, these giant fronds where I hobble, listen, fall, rise, listen and hobble on, wondering sometimes . . . if I shall ever see again the hated light, at least unloved, stretched palely between the last boles, and my mother, to settle with her, and if I would not do better, at least just as well, to hang myself from a bough, with a liane. For frankly light meant nothing to me now . . . [*Molloy*, p. 105-6].

The fact that Molloy feels a compulsion, his 'imperatives,' to keep on and to find his mother in spite of the realization that 'light meant nothing to me now' reflects the same type of irrational compulsion to consciousness and to a knowledge that is no knowledge which was seen to govern the Unnamable in the preceding chapter of this study. It is significant that this realization in Molloy is accompanied by the thought of suicide, of hanging himself 'from a bough, with a liane.' As he realizes that a simple awareness of the emptiness of knowledge does not free him from the compulsion to go on trying to know, he sees death as the only possible deliverance.

Moran also has a desire to die, and it seems to have been with him for a long time. The reader will remember a reference in the previous chapter to the graveyard near Moran's house in which he has his 'plot in perpetuity.' He evidently has owned this grave for some time before that fateful August Sunday on which he receives the call to pursue Molloy, since in leaving his garden late that night to set forth, one of the things he thinks of with

nostalgia and also with a certain amount of satisfaction is the grave
that lies prepared for him. The manner in which he describes it
betrays an impatience to occupy it :

> Sometimes I went and looked at my grave. The stone was up
> already. It was a simple Latin cross, white. I wanted to have
> my name put on it, with the here lies and the date of my birth.
> Then all it would have wanted was the date of my death. They
> would not let me. Sometimes I smiled, as if I were dead already
> [*Molloy*, p. 185].

Apparently the world has weighed heavily on Moran's shoulders
for some time, even before the quest for Molloy and the fall of
his old idols, Youdi and the God of Christianity; and the loss
of his home and possessions takes away the few comforts he once
had in life. With these losses the longing for death becomes still
more intense. Consequently the thought of suicide begins to occupy
his mind. Having built a fire one night for warmth he thinks how
nice it would be if it would burn him to death : '. . . in the end,
overcome with heat and weariness, I lay down on the ground near
the fire and fell asleep, saying, Perhaps a spark will set fire to my
clothes and I wake a living torch' (p. 201). One of the theological
questions he puzzles over on his way home has to do with an
acceptable means to suicide : '17. What would I do until my
death? Was there no means of hastening this, without falling into
a state of sin? (p. 231).' A statement Moran makes during the
course of his narrative reflecting his state of mind at the time of
writing shows that what he longs for is not simply physical death
but a release from the burdens of activity and thought. He describes how pleasant it would be to lie totally paralyzed and sense-
less, free from his compulsions to travel and to think :

> To be literally incapable of motion at last that must be some-
> thing! My mind swoons when I think of it. And mute into the
> bargain! And perhaps as deaf as a post! And who knows as
> blind as a bat! And as likely as not your memory a blank!
> And just enough brain intact to allow you to exult! And to
> dread death like a regeneration [*Molloy*, p. 192].

Moran wants to become free from those features of life that
make it a burden—and at this point in his career they constitute

practically all of life as he knows it—but death itself remains an object of fear.

Moran's dread of death probably derives from a simple reluctance to trust the unknown. Molloy, describing his idea of death, also expresses feelings of this sort :

> . . . death is a condition I have never been able to conceive to my satisfaction and which therefore cannot go down in the ledger of weal and woe. . . . Yes, the confusion of my ideas on the subject of death was such that I sometimes wondered, believe me or not, if it wasn't a state of being even worse than life. So I found it natural not to rush into it and, when I forgot myself to the point of trying, to stop in time [*Molloy*, p. 91].

He does, however, sometimes forget himself to the point of trying, and not only on the occasion mentioned above when he thinks of hanging himself from a bough. At one point he even makes a half-hearted attempt to cut his wrist :

> I took the vegetable knife from my pocket and set about opening my wrist. But pain soon got the better of me. First I cried out, then I gave up, closed the knife and put it back in my pocket. I wasn't particularly disappointed, in my heart of hearts I had not hoped for anything better [*Molloy*, p. 82].

Like Moran, Molloy has apparently been preoccupied with a desire for death for a long time. Speaking of his liaison with Edith-Ruth some years earlier he says that when he met her he was 'bent double over a heap of muck, in the hope of finding something to disgust me for ever with eating' (p. 77), and when he killed Lousse's dog by running him over with his bicycle, he reflected that the dog was more fortunate than he : '. . . he at least was dead' (p. 46).

There seems to be something like a desire for the cessation of thought and activity in the desire Molloy feels at one point to be rid of his testicles, a traditional symbol of vitality. At the end of his description of how they encumbered him, 'dangling at mid-thigh at the end of a meagre cord,' getting in his way when he walked and bouncing up and down when he rode his bicycle, he concludes : 'So the best thing for me would have been for them to go, and I would have seen to it myself, with a knife or secateurs, but for my terror of physical pain and festered wounds . . .' (p. 47). His reluctance to undergo the pain of the operation is probably not the only reason for his unwillingness to part with them. The same ambivalence operates in Molloy's case that was noticed in Moran's, a simultaneous longing and reluctance to escape from life. Consequently it is with a feeling of some perplexity that he adds : 'But those cullions, I must be attached to them after all, cherish them as others do their scars, or the family album.' He doesn't know why he should continue to feel attached to something he would rather be rid of, but the attachment remains. The same attachment to the kind of vitality that testicles represent probably figures in his motives for giving a beating to the charcoal-burner he meets later in the forest.

> People imagine, because you are old, poor, crippled, terrified, that you can't stand up for yourself, and generally speaking that is so. But given favourable conditions, a feeble and awkward assailant, in your own class what, and a lonely place, and you have a good chance of showing what stuff you are made of [*Molloy*, p. 114].

In another instance, it is a more specifically mental type of life with which he is reluctant to part, but it is probably the same divided state of mind that is operative. Much as he would like to be relieved of the burden of consciousness, he keeps thinking just to reassure himself that he still has the mental existence he so dislikes :

> For my part I willingly asked myself questions, one after the other, just for the sake of looking at them. No, not willingly, wisely, so that I might believe I was still there. And yet it meant nothing to me to be still there. I called that thinking. I thought almost without stopping, I did not dare stop [*Molloy*, p. 66].

The idea of death inspires a similarly ambivalent reaction in Malone, who is waiting to die with both eagerness and reluctance. In the very first sentence of his text he introduces the theme of death : 'I shall soon be quite dead at last in spite of all'; and he seems to think it curious that he does nothing to hasten his death :

'I could die today, if I wished, merely by making an effort, if I could wish, if I could make an effort. But it is just as well to let myself die quietly, without rushing things. Something must have changed' (*Malone*, p. 1). He even, to his surprise, finds himself feeling what might be called a normal human attachment to life : 'For the past few days I have been finding something attractive about everything' (p. 4). This feeling persists even to the end, to the last words Malone speaks concerning himself :

> All is pretext, Sapo and the birds, Moll, the peasants . . . pretext for not coming to the point, the abandoning, the raising of the arms and going down, without further splash. . . . Yes, there is no good pretending, it is hard to leave everything [*Malone*, p. 107].

Still, death also remains attractive to him, and in many places he expresses a real distaste for life. Although he says on page 22 that all he asks is that the last of his stories 'should have living for its theme,' the stories he tells tend more to have death for their theme. Malone's principal character, Macmann, has little interest in living, and it is only for reasons obscure to him that he bothers to go on doing what is necessary to keep himself alive :

> . . . indeed he had devoted to these little tasks a great part of his existence. . . . For he had to, he had to, if he wished to go on coming and going on the earth, which to tell the truth he did not, particularly, but he had to, for obscure reasons known who knows to God alone . . . [*Malone*, p. 72].

Macmann's nurse, Moll, seems to hint at suicide when she says she wants the two of them to die together, adding darkly, 'In any case I have the key to the medicine cupboard' (p. 90). And Malone not only talks about suicide through the mouths of his characters, he also speaks of it in his own right. On page 44, for example, he says, 'If I had the use of my body I would throw it out of the window,' though the very next sentence reveals the other side of his divided attitude, his reluctance to 'leave everything' : 'But perhaps it is the knowledge of my impotence that emboldens me to that thought.'

It may be that his deepest reason for being reluctant to die is the fear that death alone would bring no relief from his real burden, which is not physical existence but mental, conscious existence. This is apparently what he means on the following page : 'There is naturally another possibility that does not escape me, though it would be a great disappointment to have it confirmed, and that is that I am dead already and that all continues more or less as when I was not' (*Malone*, p. 45). Nevertheless, his awareness of the possibility that death might not actually solve his problem does not prevent him from continuing to place some hope in it. Thirty-seven pages later, still thinking of the attractiveness of death, he says that one of the advantages of trying to move his bed would be that 'the physical effort may polish me off, by means of heart failure' (p. 82).

The main advantage, however, to moving the bed would be, he says, that 'while thus employed I shall stop telling myself lies.' Here again he realizes that his real problem is his compulsion to keep thinking and writing. Close to the end of the book he expresses the same idea with a still clearer sense of realization when he says of the exercise-book in which he writes his stories : 'This exercise-book is my life, this big child's exercise-book, it has taken me a long time to resign myself to that,' but even here he finds it necessary to add, 'And yet I shall not throw it away' (p. 105).

There are occasions on which Malone is temporarily delivered from the necessity to be conscious. His reaction to this when it happens is one of rejoicing : 'And during all this time, so fertile in incidents and mishaps, in my head I suppose all was streaming and emptying away as through a sluice, to my great joy, until finally nothing remained, either of Malone or of the other' (*Malone*, p. 50). At the beginning of the book when he is telling the reader that he does not know how he arrived in his present room, Malone is not absolutely certain he lost consciousness during the trip, but even to have lost the memory of a certain period of consciousness seems fortunate to him :

I do not remember how I got here. In an ambulance perhaps, a vehicle of some kind certainly. One day I found myself here, in the bed. Having probably lost consciousness somewhere, I benefit by a hiatus in my recollections, not to be resumed until I recovered my senses, in this bed [*Malone*, p. 5].

He realizes, however, the temporary character of these moments of release and the tenacity of his mental activity. On page 114, comparing his process of dying to a birth into death, he says, 'The feet are clear already of the great cunt of existence,' but adds, 'My head will be the last to die.'

Like Moran and Molloy, Malone also uses imagery of light and darkness to express his feelings about consciousness, but where Molloy was more conscious of a loathing for light, Malone, at least in the beginning of his book, is more aware of a fear of darkness. For Molloy the darkness is relatively farther away, perhaps more of an abstraction, but for Malone it is an intense reality which he can keep at a distance only by the constant activity of his mind. Now, bedridden as he is, the only mental activity available is story-telling. He has tried this method before, but with only limited success :

> I turned on all the lights, I took a good look all round, I began to play with what I saw. People and things ask nothing better than to play, certain animals too. All went well at first, they all came to me, pleased that someone should want to play with them. . . . But it was not long before I found myself alone in the dark [*Malone*, p. 2].

Through most of his life after that he stumbled around in the dark 'with outstretched arms,' but now he is resolved to try again to distract himself from the darkness by telling stories—'From now on it will be different. I shall never do anything any more from now on but play' (pp. 2-3)—though he realizes that this may be no more than a partially successful diversion.

In his stories also he wishes to avoid darkness. Speaking of the story of Sapo which he is just beginning, he says on page 13 :

> I want as little as possible of darkness in his story. A little dark-ness, in itself, at the time, is nothing. You think no more about it and you go on. But I know what darkness is, it accumulates, thickens, then suddenly bursts and drowns everything.

And in telling he resolves to avoid to the best of his ability the use of certain phrases that threaten him with the same darkness by undermining what little confidence in reason he has left : 'I know those little phrases that seem so innocuous and, once you let them in, pollute the whole of speech. *Nothing is more real than nothing.* They rise up out of the pit and know no rest until they drag you down into its dark' (*Malone*, p. 16).

It seems surprising, then, to move from this statement on page 16 to another that directly contradicts it on page 17. Malone distinguishes between himself and his character on the basis that Sapo spent his time looking for light and took no pleasure in darkness: 'Nothing is less like me than this patient, reasonable child, struggling all alone for years to shed a little light upon himself, avid of the least gleam, a stranger to the joys of darkness' (p. 17). The apparent contradiction is only verbal, however, since both statements are true with respect to the speaker. They only make more vivid the divided state of mind of Malone, who has spent his life as he is now, compelled toward the light and reluctantly fleeing it.

Malone is not consistent in his account of Sapo's feelings about light and darkness either. Only ten pages after the statement in which he said Sapo was a stranger to 'the joys of darkness,' Malone says Sapo sometimes sought relief from the light by turning to darkness:

> . . . Sapo, his face turned towards an earth so resplendent that it hurt his eyes, felt at his back and all about him the unconquerable dark, and it licked the light on his face. Sometimes abruptly he turned to face it, letting it envelop and pervade him, with a kind of relief [*Malone*, p. 27].

Immediately before these lines there is a description of how the light came through the door and window of the room Sapo is sitting in, a room in the Lamberts' cottage. From this it would seem that the light being talked about is simply physical light, but that the light is also, in Sapo's, or Malone's associations, the light of consciousness and life, and that the darkness represents unconsciousness and death is clear from the lines that immediately follow:

> But silence was in the heart of the dark, the silence of dust and the things that would never stir, if left alone. And the ticking of the invisible alarm-clock was as the voice of that silence which, like the dark, would one day triumph too. And then all would be still and dark and all things at rest for ever at last.

Perhaps the reason for this inconsistency in Sapo is that Malone is really talking about himself indirectly and that he is more concerned with expressing his own feelings about life than with creating a consistent character. If this is true, the equanimity with which Sapo is supposed to travel through the world of ignorance and deceptive knowledge, 'passing from light to shadow, from shadow to light, unheedingly' (p. 30), may actually represent an ideal of indifference or *ataraxia* that Malone himself would like to achieve. And perhaps also when Lemuel glares 'with loathing at the sun' (p. 111), he expresses Malone's own feelings of longing for a final deliverance from the light.

The battle between light and darkness for the allegiance of Malone never ends. Much as he longs for deliverance from thought throughout his volume, cries for light appear among his last fragmentary utterances (p. 120):

> or light light I mean
> never there he will never
> never anything
> there
> any more

If the Unnamable is in fact as he appears to be, a post mortem state of Malone, the ambivalence with which he longed for and yet held back from silence, darkness, and death has been replaced by a disillusionment with death and an unequivocal desire for release from the necessity of consciousness. He has passed through death and found it lacking, but he still longs for what he had hoped death would bring him. Occasionally he falls back into the old habit of wishing he were dead, as when he says on page 34, 'I hope I may be—I nearly said hanged, but that I hope in any case. . . .' When he speaks of the hope of ending, however—'Yes, it is to be wished, to end would be wonderful, no matter who I am, no matter where I am' (*Unnamable*, p. 19)—he is thinking not of physical death but of that which he had previously hoped for from it, the end of the compulsion endlessly to go on thinking.

Like the others, the Unnamable also uses light imagery to express his attitude toward consciousness. Although he speaks at one point with contempt of this very way of thinking, 'What rubbish all this stuff about light and dark. And how I have luxuriated in

it' (p. 24), he goes on using it in his stories in the same manner
as always. Speculating on the reasons for the persistence of consciousness, he makes up the hypothesis that there are tormentors
who are assigned the duty of keeping him conscious by speaking
through him. At one point he imagines they have gone away 'in
Indian file, casting long shadows, towards their master' (p. 108),
who would seem to be a kind of sun, that is, the light of consciousness causing them to cast long shadows as they approach
him. Then he speculates that they have arranged to maintain
him in consciousness even in their absence by leaving behind them
their lamps :

> . . . their powerful lamps, lit and trained on the within, to make
> him think they are still there, notwithstanding the silence, or
> to make him think the grey is natural, or to make him go on
> suffering, for he does not suffer from the noise alone, he suffers
> from the grey too, from the light . . . [*Unnamable*, p. 109].

In this passage 'they' represent voices, consciousness in the form
of articulated processes of thought. The lights they leave behind
and perhaps the sun, their master, seem to represent a kind of
contentless, or at least nonconceptual, pure awareness. But the
distinction between the two types of consciousness is only tentative
on the part of the Unnamable, who finds the whole problem very
difficult to understand or describe, and the very fact that he goes
on talking about this would indicate that the voices have not really
stopped. For the most part, consciousness for the trilogy and for
the Unnamable is cogitative process : thought and awareness are
almost indistinguishable. The closeness of their relationship can
be seen from another passage in which the two images of light and
the voice merge : 'Ah if only this voice could stop, this meaningless voice which prevents you from being nothing, just barely
prevents you from being nothing and nowhere, just enough to keep
alight this little yellow flame . . .' (pp. 116-17).

Besides the imagery of light and darkness, another type of
imagery that Malone and the Unnamable use in connection with
their desires to escape from consciousness is that of birth. In the
case of Malone, who still places great hope in death, it takes the
form of images of birth into death.[2] He says that his closeness to
death makes him feel 'far already from the world that parts at

last its labia and lets me go' (p. 12). Toward the end of his account, as he feels death drawing closer still, he thinks of the room he lives in as a womb beginning to labor in the travail of birth : 'The ceiling rises and falls, rises and falls, rhythmically, as when I was a foetus. . . . I am being given, if I may venture the expressions, birth to [*sic*] into death, such is my impression' (*Malone*, p. 114). Another use of the same image introduces another theme which will take on great importance in the case of the Unnamable, that of the necessity of being born in order to die :

> Be born, that's the brainwave now, that is to say live long enough to get acquainted with free carbonic gas, then say thanks for the nice time and go. . . . Yes, an old foetus, that's what I am now, hoar and impotent, mother is done for, I've rotted her, she'll drop me with the help of gangrene, perhaps papa is at the party too, I'll land head-foremost mewling in the charnelhouse . . . [*Malone*, p. 51].

The Unnamable, on the other side of physical death, realizes the falseness of the hope Malone placed in it. For him the state he is in now, cut off from all distractions such as possessions and other external concerns, is far worse than the type of life Moran, Molloy, and Malone suffered from. He still speaks of the hope of dying, but what he means by 'death' is mental silence. Trying to understand how to reach this silence, he speculates that perhaps the reason 'they' continue to torment him with their voices and lights is that they are trying to get him to live in some fuller manner before they will leave him alone. Often he speaks of the necessity of being born again in order really to live and thereby to become eligible for a complete death. He has already left several incomplete lives by means of incomplete deaths which brought him no rest :

> But say I succeed in dying, to adopt the most comforting hypothesis, without having been able to believe I ever lived, I know to my cost it is not that they wish for me. For it has happened to me many times already, without their having granted me as much as a brief sick-leave among the worms, before resurrecting me [*Unnamable*, p. 76].

He realizes that a simple death in the identity of Worm, the creature in the jar, is not what they really want from him, but he is completely at a loss as to what they do want. One possibility is that they want him to identify completely with some character, and he thinks about this idea at great length. In fact, it recurs continually during the last hundred pages. He feels that what went wrong was that his identification with Worm was only partial :

> If only I knew what they want, they want me to be Worm, but I was, I was, what's wrong, I was, but ill, it must be that, it can only be that, what else can it be, but that, I didn't report in the light, the light of day, in their midst to hear them say, Didn't we tell you you were alive and kicking? [*Unnamable*, p. 107].

His greatest difficulty is that he does not know how to go about getting born into a wholehearted identification with a character. He would be willing if he only knew how : 'Another trap to snap me up among the living. It's how to fall into it they can't have explained to me sufficiently. They'll never get the better of my stupidity' (p. 81).

If trapping him in an identity is indeed what they want, they are a persistent group, for they never give up. They even employ what sounds like the techniques of high-pressure salesmanship to persuade him to accept their product :

> But my dear man, come, be reasonable, look, this is you, look at this photograph, and here's your file, no convictions, I assure you, come now, make an effort, at your age, to have no identity, it's a scandal, I assure you, look at this photograph . . . [*Unnamable*, p. 125].

Their main selling point is that accepting an identity is the only way he will be able to die : '. . . look, here's the photograph, you'll see, you'll be all right, what does it amount too [*sic*], after all, a painful moment, on the surface, then peace, underneath, it's the only way, believe me, the only way out . . .' (*Unnamable*, p. 126). And when the Unnamable is still resistant, they try him with another potential identity, the most attractive feature of which is the prospect of a short life :

. . . have I nothing else, why certainly, certainly, just a
second . . . yes, I was right, no doubt about it this time, it's
you all over, look, here's the photograph, take a look at that,
dying on his feet, you'd better hurry, it's a bargain, I assure
you . . . [*Unnamable*, p. 126].

Again, the Unnamable would be willing to cooperate with them
so as to achieve the silence their offers imply, but he does not know
how : '. . . they don't understand, I can't stir, they think I don't
want to, that their conditions don't suit me . . . I can't go to them,
they'll have to come and get me if they want me . . .' (p. 127). They
even try him with the idea of being born as the sperm from an
adolescent's nocturnal emission, but with no more success :

. . . here comes another . . what a hope, the bright boy is there
. . . some people are lucky, born of a wet dream and dead before
morning, I must say I'm tempted, no, the testis has yet to
descend that would want any truck with me, it's mutual, another
gleam down the drain [*Unnamable*, p. 129].

Actually the Unnamable is not at all certain what sort of birth
it is that he has to undergo in order to be eligible for a final death.
That he has to become completely identified with one of the
characters he talks about is only one possible interpretation of
this 'birth.' Another possibility that occurs to him is that his inability
to achieve silence may be due to some obscure moral failure on
his part, the failure to fulfill an obligation to speak with his own
voice for a change instead of through the mouths of characters.
He knows that 'they' are trying to persuade him to identify with
one of the characters, but he also suspects that their master wants
something else, that he wants the Unnamable to speak about
himself : 'For beyond them is that other who will not give me
quittance until they have abandoned me as inutilizable and restored
me to myself. Then at last I can set about saying what I was, and
where, during all this long lost time' (*Unnamable*, p. 60).

If this is the real problem, then the answer is not to identify himself with his characters, but to dissociate himself from them altogether. In fact, his speaking of and through them would seem
more to be a subterfuge to avoid speaking of himself.[3] This possibility does occur to him :

> Ah yes, all lies, God and man, nature and the light of day,
> the heart's outpourings and the means of understanding, all
> invented, basely, by me alone, with the help of no one, since
> there is no one, to put off the hour when I must speak of me
> [*Unnamable*, p. 22].

In this passage he blames himself for not having spoken the words
that would bring him silence. In other places he is not sure where
the guilt lies, since he is not even sure of his own identity or of
that of the voice. In one place, for example, he blames Mahood for
having usurped his voice and thereby having prevented him from
speaking in his own right: '. . . his [Mahood's] voice continued to
testify for me, as though woven into mine, preventing me from
saying who I was, what I was, so as to have done with saying,
done with listening' (p. 29). In another place the Unnamable
speaks of the voice as though it were something completely anonymous: 'This voice that speaks, knowing that it lies, indifferent to
what it says, too old perhaps and too abased ever to succeed in
saying the words that would be its last' (p. 26).

Much of the time, however, he cannot see whose the voice could
be if not his. Consequently he feels a gnawing sense of guilt at the
innate duplicity that will never let him speak the truth about
himself, which prevents him at every turn from 'saying something
at last that is not false, if that is what they want, so as to have
nothing more to say' (p. 47).

Why he is required to speak of himself, what he would be
expected to say, or how this could possibly set him free are all
mysteries to him. All he knows is that he is 'in a daze of baseless
unanswerable self-reproach' (p. 121). Sometimes he tries to reason
with himself about it :

> . . . it's not my fault, all I can say is that it's not my fault, it's
> not anyone's fault, since there isn't anyone it can't be anyone's
> fault, since there isn't anyone but me it can't be mine, sometimes
> you'd think I was reasoning . . . [*Unnamable*, p. 162].

It is not, however, a matter which falls in the province of reason.
It has an irrational validity of its own. Realizing this, he can only
conclude: '. . . all here is sin, you don't know why, you don't
know whose, you don't know against whom . . .' (p. 164).

At the very end of the volume, on the last page the Unnamable is still plagued by the same irrational sense of guilt : '. . . you must go on, I'll go on, you must say words, as long as there are any, until they find me, until they say me, strange pain, strange sin . . .' (p. 179). His reasons for these feelings of guilt are as mysterious to the reader as they are to him. Driven to try to understand his situation and to find a way out of it, he makes up explanations only to reject them and then make them up all over again. The whole idea of guilt and punishment may be only a hypothesis with no real relevance, one more thought produced by consciousness in its endless necessity to fill up the silence : '. . . . you must go on, I can't go on, I'll go on.'

CHAPTER VIII

Inferno

As the characters of the trilogy come to find themselves trapped in an endless necessity to keep going on, moving or thinking or both, they come to see time as an 'enormous prison' (*Unnamable*, p. 171). The earlier characters, who still retain some hope that time is moving toward a goal, do not fully realize that there is no escape. As this realization dawns on them and becomes fully conscious in the Unnamable, time ceases to appear to have a direction; it is seen finally as either a monotonous repetition of the same patterns or simply an eternal present, the reality of which can only be described as hell.

To the earlier characters, Moran, Molloy, and Malone, linear time, the kind of time that appears to be passing and moving in some direction, seems to be both their greatest affliction and their greatest hope. As time passes, it leads them through progressive degrees of physical decrepitude as well as through a painful series of excoriations of personality in which they are carried deeper and deeper into the knowledge of the emptiness and absurdity of life, but it also appears to them to be leading toward a death which, although it frightens them, offers the hope of peace.

The hope of escape is difficult to outgrow. Malone at one point speaks with scorn of the idea that time is moving toward an end—'I used not to know where I was going, but I knew I would arrive, I knew there would be an end to the long blind road. What half-truths, my God' (*Malone*, p. 4)—but he still hopes that death will take him 'beyond this tumult' to 'a great calm, and a great indifference, never really to be troubled by anything again' (p. 22).

Molloy, apparently anticipating the condition of the Unnamable beyond his present state and his next state as Malone, had expressed the hope that there the series would end : 'This time, then once more I think, then perhaps a last time, then I think it'll be over, with that world too' (*Molloy*, p. 8). Neither Molloy nor Malone is right; there is no end and no great calm on the other side.

The Unnamable realizes, as none of the previous characters fully did, that time is not moving toward anything, that linear time is a delusion that he has imposed on himself in order not to have to face the real hopelessness of life :

> All this business of a labour to accomplish, before I can end, of words to say . . . before I can be done with speaking, done with listening, I invented it all, in the hope it would console me . . . allow me to think of myself as somewhere on a road, moving, between a beginning and an end . . . [*Unnamable*, pp. 35-36].

And he goes on to describe the time he now finds himself in as a 'labyrinthine torment that can't be grasped, or limited. . . .' Time is not a road moving toward a goal but a labyrinth in which one wanders lost, around and around.

The earlier characters of the trilogy showed at times a dim, slowly growing awareness that the real direction of time's movement was not forward in a straight line but in circles. Moran touches upon this idea when he says on page 125 that his son will someday go through experiences closely similar to his. He hardly has any idea that the frustrating patterns of time will be repeated not only in the life of his son but also in his own, but that the time he himself moves through is cyclical is symbolized by the round of the year that encompasses his journey, bringing him back to his home again at the same time of year that he had earlier left it : 'It is summer again. This time a year ago I was setting out' (*Molloy*, p. 240).

Molloy, too, moves through the year's cycle. He says that he set out in June, and he believes, though with less certainty than Moran, that it 'must have been' (p. 123) a spring morning when he finally emerged from the forest. Although Molloy's sense of time is less sure than Moran's, his understanding of the circularity of time and of what this means in his own life is more advanced. 'Whatever I do,' he says on page 61 of his section, '. . . it will always as it were be the same thing.' And the antipathy he was described in the last chapter as feeling toward the light of the sun as a symbol of consciousness may also have involved a certain hostility toward the sun itself as a symbol of cyclical time.

Malone has even less definite a sense of the seasons he is passing through than does Molloy, though he is very much aware of the relentlessness and repetitiousness of their cycles: 'Thus with the year Seasons return' (*Malone*, p. 33). As the characters of the trilogy advance toward the utter confusion of the Unnamable, they lose their grasp of the passage of time, even as their understanding of time's cyclical quality increases. Malone speaks of the stars as 'absurd lights' (p. 119), and he says that he cannot make sense of them, but the circular patterns the moon moves through stand out clearly: 'The moon on the other hand has grown familiar, I am well familiar now with her changes of aspect and orbit . . .' (p. 7). In his case, however, the moon's cyclical movements suggest not only dreariness but also hope. Malone, who feels very close to death, sees in the moon a symbol of the death he hopes to find. He describes the moon as a 'dead world, airless, waterless' (p. 26), and he hopes that if he will have any existence after this life it will be like that of the moon, completely dead and unconscious: To be dead, before her, on her, with her, and turn, dead on dead, about poor mankind, and never have to die anymore . . .' (p. 93).

Somewhat as he had wished, Malone, in *The Unnamable*, is turning about poor mankind. Like the moon, he 'appears and disappears with the punctuality of clockwork' (*Unnamable*, p. 7). If, however, as appears to be the case, Malone is simply one of the many personalities that have been worn for a while and then sloughed off by the Unnamable, his end is not all he had hoped it would be. His consciousness has not died; it is simply carried on in the Unnamable himself, who is still driven by the same necessity as ever to keep on going 'in perpetual motion, accompanied by Malone, as the earth by its moon' (p. 9).

Deprived of all hope of ever arriving anywhere, the Unnamable sees all his movements as roughly circular. In his abortive life as Mahood, the one-legged traveler, he first journeys about the earth in a great circle and then returns to his home, where he circles about his family : 'So we turned, in our respective orbits, I without, they within' (p. 41). Shortly after this he says, 'To go on, I still call that on, to go on and get on has been my only care, if not always in a straight line, at least in obedience to the figure assigned to me' (p. 45). And the figure assigned seems at present to be 'a succession of irregular loops' (p. 54).

When he says sardonically of the idea of going on, 'I still call that on,' he means that he realizes that although he finds himself compelled to keep moving, at least in the personalities he has to adopt, movement is a strange term for it, since it leads him nowhere. Later he realizes that his thoughts too, even when he is not imagining himself as a person moving through space, are carrying him over and over the same ground : 'I have passed by here, this has passed by me, thousands of times, its turn has come again, it will pass on and something else will be there, another instant of my old instant' (p. 158). All instants are the same instant, endlessly repeated, and therefore time, moving through circular patterns, is actually standing still. Although the Unnamable cannot help talking in temporal categories—'There are no days here, but I use the expression' (p. 5)—he comes to see time as just another one of the illusions that 'they' have imposed on him : '. . . they've inflicted the notion of time on me too' (p. 52). The time that moves both him and all mankind through endlessly repeated patterns of illusion and frustration is not itself in movement from nor to anywhere :

> . . . the question may be asked, off the record, why time doesn't pass, doesn't pass from you, why it piles up all about you, instant on instant, on all sides, deeper and deeper, thicker and thicker, your time, others' time, the time of the ancient dead and the dead yet unborn, why it buries you grain by grain neither dead nor alive . . . [p. 143].

The only reality is the 'labouring whirl' (p. 161) in which 'the seconds' are 'all alike and each one is infernal' (p. 152).

To see that all time is a single infernal moment is to see that life itself is something that can only be adequately described as a hell. The Unnamable is the first character to realize this fully. Hell, a traditional Christian concept, is only an analogy, of course, as the Unnamable knows, but he finds himself forced to employ

it because it seems to be the least inadequate of the analogies he
could apply to his situation. He is uneasy with it, but he cannot
escape using it. At one point he tries to reject the entire idea as
just one more of the illusory patterns which his compulsive ratiocina-
tion makes him impose on the universe : 'Set aside once and for
all . . . the analogy with orthodox damnation . . .' (p. 144). Much
as he would like to, however, he cannot set aside the analogy
with the Christian hell, any more than he can stop thinking. Only
four pages later he does not even notice that he is using it again :
'. . . strange mixture of solid and liquid, a little air now is all we
need to complete the elements, no, I'm forgetting fire, unusual
hell when you come to think of it . . .' (p. 148). Somewhat later
still he thinks it may be the devil who is behind the thinking that
torments him : '. . . who can have come here, the devil perhaps, I
can think of no one else, it's he showed me everything, here, in
the dark, and how to speak, and what to say . . .' (pp. 166-67).

It is difficult to conceptualize a universe that is actually meaningless, but, compelled to keep trying to find ways to understand the unintelligible, the characters of the trilogy are forced to try to find
analogies to describe the pain and the absurdity of their lives,
and since they share an Irish Catholic background, they find
traditional Christian imagery the most readily available for this
purpose.

Although there are occasional uses of other types of Christian
imagery in *The Unnamable*, such as references to stigmata (p. 38),
to 'the thorns they'll have to come and stick into me, as into their
unfortunate Jesus' (p. 87), and to unwanted resurrections that make
the Unnamable begin talking again every time he hopes he has
gone silent, the most elaborately developed Christian image in
the last volume is that of hell. This is the most suitable image for
a person who finds himself stuck in a miserable situation with no
hope of exit. The earlier characters, on the other hand, have not
yet reached the level of despair from which the Unnamable views
the human condition, and consequently the imagery they use to
describe their own lives tends to be slightly different. To characters
like Moran and Molloy, who are in incessant movement, the most
suitable image seems to be the *via dolorosa*, the way of the cross.
Both liken themselves to Christ carrying the cross or to Christ
crucified on it.

Moran does not develop the imagery of the cross as elaborately as does Molloy, perhaps because his sense of life's horror and his realization of its absurdity are less advanced. Occasionally, however, he does use such imagery, as when referring to the stiffness that has set in in his leg, he says, 'New as this new cross was I at once found the most comfortable way of being crushed' (p. 191). On page 202, likening his very existence to a perpetual crucifixion, he says that it was less uncomfortable for him to stand leaning on his umbrella 'than when I stood supported only by my muscles and the tree of life,' a powerfully concise image into which he compresses both the tree of life of the garden of Eden and the life-giving tree of Calvary.

Molloy, by means of various Christian allusions throughout his narrative, makes of his entire life a sort of inverse parallel to the life of Christ, a negative commentary on the Christian hope. His meaning is that instead of the Holy Infant born of a pure virgin, there is only a person like Molloy born of a 'poor old uniparous whore' (p. 23), and instead of the saving crucifixion of Christ, there is only the meaningless crucifixion of Molloy, with resurrection not a triumph but the ultimate defeat. Toward the beginning of his story, Molloy mentions the incarnation of Christ and the Angelus, a devotion to Christ's mother, in the same breath in which he recounts his decision to go and see his own mother: '. . . having waked between eleven o'clock and midday (I heard the angelus, recalling the incarnation, shortly after) I resolved to go and see my mother' (p. 19). He does not make the analogy of himself to Christ any more explicit than this, but the parallel is called to the attention of the reader implicitly by the juxtaposition of Christ's mother and of Molloy's. This juxtaposition in thought having been made, the reader cannot help, a few pages later, comparing the traditional picture of Christ, simultaneously the terminus of the Hebrew dispensation and the beginning of the Christian, himself both God and man, with Molloy's description of himself as 'the last of my foul brood, neither man nor beast' (p. 23). Where Christ was the first figure of a renewed creation, Molloy is the ultimate achievement of a hopeless universe.

Christ is supposed to have sought his crucifixion in the hope of resurrection, but Molloy thinks of crucifixion only as the means to death. On page 34, for example, when he lies down in the cruciform position, what seem to be faint suggestions of the possibility of resurrection are unpleasant to him: 'I lay at full stretch, with outspread arms ['*les bras en croix*' in the French text, p. 38]. The white hawthorn stooped towards me, unfortunately I don't like the smell of hawthorn.' The hawthorn is a traditional symbol of spring and, by implication, of renewal and resurrection. By the third volume, the Unnamable has actually experienced with bitterness that of which Molloy only has faintly disagreeable intimations. He says that he has already died several times 'without their having granted me as much as a brief sick-leave among the worms, before resurrecting me' (*Unnamable*, p. 76). Less experienced and less disillusioned than the Unnamable, Molloy still thinks of death as offering a possibility of peace, and for this reason crucifixion takes on in his imagination a desirable quality, though as was seen in the preceding chapter, an irrational instinct of self-preservation always keeps death beyond his reach. Crucifixion is a goal he desires but which always eludes him, and the image which seems to him to most adequately sum up his life is that of an endless *via dolorosa*, 'a veritable calvary, with no limit to its stations and no hope of crucifixion' (p. 105).

Malone, a more nearly stationary character than either Moran or Molloy, concentrates his attention on the crucifixion itself rather than on the *via dolorosa*. There are two places in his stories in which crucifixes appear. The first is on page 39, where he describes the Lamberts' furnishings as including a crucifix hanging from a nail. This would be an expected fixture in any Catholic peasant's cottage, but it is probably also there as an element in the structure of the story, a symbol of the manner in which the specter of pain and death hangs over the activities of the living.

The principal use of crucifixion imagery in *Malone Dies* is in the figure of Moll. After Malone has already made Moll into a living embodiment of grotesque sexuality by descriptions of her intercourse with Macmann and of the amatory letters and macabre love-poetry they exchange, he enlarges her still further into a symbol of life itself, combining in one figure both the enticements and the horror of life and intermingling the conflicting attractions of both life and death :

One day, just as Macmann was getting used to being loved, though without as yet responding as he was subsequently to do, he thrust Moll's face away from his on the pretext of examining her ear-rings. But as she made to return to the charge he checked

her again with the first words that came into his head, namely,
Why two Christs?, implying that in his opinion one was more
than sufficient. To which she made the absurd reply, Why two
ears? But she obtained his forgiveness a moment later, saying,
with a smile (she smiled at the least thing), Besides they are
the thieves, Christ is in my mouth. Then parting her jaws and
pulling down her blobber-lip she discovered, breaking with its
solitary fang the monotony of the gums, a long yellow canine
bared to the roots and carved, with the drill probably, to represent the celebrated sacrifice [*Malone*, p. 93].

The image of the two thieves seems to represent the manner in
which life continually torments its victims with illusory hopes—
'why be discouraged, one of the thieves was saved, that is a
generous percentage' (p. 83)—but the central image, an integral
part of the very mouth with which Moll kisses her lover, is the
cross of Christ, the traditional symbol of the most intense suffering.

To Macmann, and to his creator, Malone, however, crucifixion
appears to offer, in addition to suffering, the possibility of death, an
end to suffering, and it is probably the alluringness of death which,
uniting with the enticements of Eros, makes Macmann find such
appeal in Moll's tooth :

This incident made a strong impression on Macmann and Moll
rose with a bound in his affections. And in the pleasure he was
later to enjoy, when he put his tongue in her mouth and let it
wander over her gums, this rotten crucifix had assuredly its
part [*Malone*, p. 93].

Malone seems to be projecting into Macmann his own hopes for
escape. Crucifixion and death can seem final and therefore hopeful
to Malone only because he has not yet had the opportunity to
become disillusioned with the idea of finality. The Unnamable,
on the other side of that supposedly final experience, knows that
that hope too, like all others, is a false dream. The only reality, for
the earlier characters as well as for the Unnamable, is an endless
hell; the difference is that he knows it more clearly than they.

The third volume of the trilogy is the story of the Unnamable's
gradual growth in understanding of the nature of the hell he is
condemned to. Actually, its nature is very simple; it consists basically of three things : '. . . the inability to speak, the inability to be

silent, and solitude . . .' (p. 153). The first two of these have already
been discussed at length as major themes in the trilogy. Solitude
is an equally important, and equally infernal, aspect of the lives
of all the characters. Each is imprisoned within himself, partially
by his own choice, and partially by the basic difficulty of communication that separates all human beings from one another.[1]
Nor is the theme of solitude or isolation limited to the trilogy.
Like Beckett's other themes, it runs through all his novels, gradually
unfolding its full significance.

The development of this theme in *More Pricks than Kicks* was
discussed in the chapter on Beckett's early writings. *Murphy* also
touches upon the subject; though, since Murphy is concerned more
with separating himself from everything and everybody than with
communicating with others, he does not feel his solitude as painful.
The narrator points out twice that when Murphy speaks to Celia,
he tends to be so absorbed in his own train of thought that his
speech 'so far from being adapted to Celia . . . was not addressed
to her' (*Murphy*, p. 136, and see p. 139). And even Celia, who wants
very much to share Murphy's life, has similar difficulty stepping
out of her own isolation in order to reach him : ' "You don't understand," said Celia, who was not trying to follow' (p. 138). The
little love that Murphy does feel for Celia tends to manifest itself
in the form of cruelty : 'He still loved her enough to enjoy cutting
the tripes out of her occasionally' (p. 140).

Watt is less averse to company than Murphy. His problem tends
to be that communication is simply very difficult if not impossible.
Watt and Sam seem to enjoy each other's companionship as they
walk between the fences that separate their pavilions in the
asylum : 'To be together again, after so long . . . that is perhaps
something . . .' (*Watt*, p. 163). But it is probably significant that,
although Sam says they would have been more comfortable either
in his garden or in Watt's, they never think to invite each other in :
'For my garden was my garden, and Watt's garden was Watt's
garden . . .' (p. 164). And the conversations they have gradually
cease to be real communication as Watt, wrestling to try to put
his baffling experiences into words, becomes more and more en-
tangled in the convolutions of his speech. Sam says he probably
understood about 'one half of what won its way past my tympan'
(p. 169). At one time, Watt had an affair with a fishwoman, Mrs
Gorman, who, it is said, 'pleased Watt greatly' (p. 138), but they

never pursued their relationship to the point of sexual intercourse, 'for Watt had not the strength, and Mrs Gorman had not the time, indispensable to even the most perfunctory coalescence' (p. 141). After the affair is over, Watt decides that what pleased him in Mrs Gorman was probably mainly the smell of fish.

The characters of the trilogy feel their isolation more keenly than did any of Beckett's earlier protagonists. As Beckett said in his study of Proust, friendship is one of the habits that make life in an absurd universe endurable. For the characters of the trilogy, other people are a nuisance, but a nuisance that at least offers some distraction from boredom and from the insatiable curiosity that torments them. At the very beginning of the first volume Molloy's description of two travelers in the countryside introduces the theme. In the original French version the travelers' names are given as A and B (see pp. 9-20 of the French text), but in the English version they were changed to A and C, perhaps to emphasize their discontinuity,[2] for what is significant about the two is that they never have any contact apart from a superficial exchange of 'a few words,' after which they continue on their separate ways.

For Molloy, the main effect of his encounter with A and C is to make him aware of his own loneliness. What strikes Molloy about the whole scene is the solitariness of C, lost in the unfamiliar countryside : 'He looks old and it is a sorry sight to see him solitary after so many years, so many days and nights. . . . And in the end, or almost, to be abroad alone, by unknown ways, in the gathering night . . .' (*Molloy*, p. 11). The sight makes Molloy feel keenly his own solitude and almost tempts him to action in an effort to find companionship with C : '. . . I watched him recede, at grips (myself) with the temptation to get up and follow him, perhaps even to catch up with him one day, so as to know him better, be myself less lonely' (pp. 12-13). He also looks longingly after A dwindling in the distance. He is tempted to run after A too, but neither A nor C stirs him to action. Reflecting on his desire for the companionship of A, he realizes that it would be futile to follow him, for no real communion would come of it :

To get up, to get down on the road, to set off hobbling in pursuit of him, to hail him, what could be easier? He hears my cries, turns, waits for me. What is it I want? Ah that tone I know, compounded of pity, of fear, of disgust. . . . There I am

then, he leaves me, he's in a hurry. He didn't seem to be in a
hurry, he was loitering, I've already said so, but after three
minutes of me he is in a hurry, he has to hurry [*Molloy*, pp.
15-16].

After imagining this hasty departure of A, Molloy reflects on what
it means to be cut off from all human contact. His conclusion is
significant :

And once again, I am I will not say alone, no, that's not like
me, but, how shall I say, I don't know, restored to myself, no,
I never left myself, free, yes, I don't know what that means
but it's the word I mean to use, free to do what, to do nothing,
to know, but what, the laws of the mind perhaps, of my
mind. . . .

Here the theme of solitude is united with the other theme explored at such length throughout the trilogy, that of the mind
trapped within itself endlessly ruminating according to an irrational
inner necessity. This is the hell in which the characters find themselves imprisoned, and if their damnation has a moral fault at its
source, this fault must involve at least in part the choice to remain
forever alone.

After the vision of A and C has pierced Molloy with a sense of
their solitariness and of his own, a vague 'craving for a fellow'
arouses him finally to action : 'But talking of the craving for a
fellow let me observe that having waked . . . I resolved to go and
see my mother' (p. 19). Although Molloy describes his quest for
his mother as an attempt to escape from solitude, there is no
reason to suppose that finding her would offer any real hope of
this. According to the story he tells us, he has visited his mother
many times in the past without ever establishing a genuinely
sympathetic relationship with her. He has held back whatever
affection he might have had to give and has only used her for his
own ends. Consequently he has remained as alone after each
visit as he was before.

Molloy's attitude toward his isolation is as ambivalent as his
attitude toward consciousness, as can be seen from the reasons
he gives for calling his mother Mag, a single word which expresses
simultaneously his desire for a mother and his contempt for her :

. . . I called her Mag, when I had to call her something. And I called her Mag because for me, without my knowing why, the letter g abolished the syllable Ma, and as it were spat on it, better than any other letter would have done. And at the same time I satisfied a deep and doubtless unacknowledged need, the need to have a Ma, that is a mother, and to proclaim it audibly [*Molloy*, p. 21].

And escape from solitude into human fellowship seems to be what he is hinting at on page 24: '. . . with her alone, I—no, I can't say it. That is to say I could say it but I won't say it, yes I could say it easily, because it wouldn't be true.'

The only reason he ever tried to enter into communication with his mother seems to have been to get money :

I got into communication with her by knocking on her skull. One knock meant yes, two no, three I don't know, four money, five goodbye. . . . That she should confuse yes, no, I don't know and goodbye, was all the same to me, I confused them myself. But that she should associate the four knocks with anything but money was something to be avoided at all costs [*Molloy*, p. 22].

He seems to have felt no concern at all with communicating affection to her. The one time he kissed her, it was reluctantly : 'Once I touched with my lips, vaguely, hastily, that little grey wizened pear. Pah (p. 24). The tone of disgust is evident. The hellishness of Molloy's solitude is hinted at somewhat later when he simultaneously disparages and affirms the need for a human relationship : 'Need of my mother ! No, there were no words for the want of need in which I was perishing' (p. 45).

Although this particular journey never does lead to his mother, he has at least one chance to come out of his isolation. The chance comes when he meets a lonely charcoal-burner in the forest. Not only does he refuse to offer his companionship to the lonely man, at the very idea of being detained he beats him brutally :

He was all over me, begging me to share his hut, believe it or not. A total stranger. Sick with solitude probably . . . when I made to go, he held me back by the sleeve. So I smartly freed a crutch and dealt him a good dint on the skull [*Molloy*, p. 113].

Then after he has turned and started to leave, he comes back and finishes the job by giving the man a few kicks in the ribs.

Moran is another who chooses to be alone, even when he feels that perhaps the inner disturbances disrupting his peace are due to excessive solitude :

> That a man like me, so meticulous and calm in the main . . .
> should let himself be haunted and possessed by chimeras . . .
> I saw it only as the weakness of a solitary, a weakness admittedly
> to be deplored, but which had to be indulged in if I wished
> to remain a solitary, and I did, I clung to that, with as little
> enthusiasm as to my hens or to my faith, but no less lucidly
> [*Molloy*, p. 156].

On the occasions when he does have the opportunity to come out of his solitude, as Molloy had with the charcoal-burner, he is completely uninterested. When Father Ambrose, for example, wants him to stay and talk a while after he administers the Communion to him, the few minutes Moran allows him seem tedious :

> I had nothing else to say to him. All I wanted was to return
> home as quickly as possible and stuff myself with stew. My soul
> appeased, I was ravenous. But being slightly in advance of my
> schedule I resigned myself to allowing him eight minutes. They
> seemed endless [*Molloy*, p. 138].

Nevertheless, Moran is tormented by solitude as much as he is by company. This inner division manifests itself clearly in his feelings toward his son. On page 166, for example, Moran says that when he tucked his son into bed, 'I was within a hair's breadth of kissing him,' though not long after this he says that he could not stand to have his son walk ahead of him when they were setting out because 'the prospect was more than I could bear of being unable to move a step without having before my eyes my son's little sullen plump body' (p. 177).

He recognizes his need for his son's companionship, but throughout his story he treats him in a way that could not fail to alienate him. When he sends his son away to buy a bicycle, he feels a sharp loneliness for him : 'The day seemed very long. I missed my son!' (p. 198). Later, after his son's return, he rejoices in being delivered from his loneliness : 'Happily the weather was fine and I no longer

alone. Happily, happily' (p. 216). Still happy as he is to have his son
back, it is not long before he has a violent quarrel with him that
drives him away permanently.

The organization that Moran works for does nothing to relieve
his solitariness. Moran would like it to be a community in which
he could find release from isolation : 'That we thought of ourselves
as members of a vast organization was doubtless also due to the
all too human feeling that trouble shared, or is it sorrow, is trouble
something, I forget the word' (p. 147). In reality this organization
is the exact opposite of a community in which the members could
share any important part of their lives with each other. All that
unites them is the fact that they are employed by Youdi to perform
certain tasks. Apart from this they have no interest in each other
or in the organization as such. When Gaber finds Moran in the
woods, intent only on delivering Youdi's orders, he pays no
attention at all to Moran's obviously desperate physical condition :

> He took a small electric torch from his pocket and shone it on
> his page. He read, Moran, Jacques, home, instanter. He put out
> his torch, closed his notebook on his finger and looked at me.
> I can't move, I said. . . . He opened his notebook again, shone
> the torch on his page, studied it at length and said, Moran,
> home, instanter. . . . Not a word on how I was looking [*Molloy*,
> p. 224].

In the French text, though not in the English for obvious reasons,
Moran comments that although he and Gaber have both been employed by Youdi for many years and have worked together as long,
they still use the formal mode of address to each other rather than
the familiar. They had tried at one time to use the familiar form,
but it didn't last : '*Nous avions essayé de nous tutoyer. En vain
Moi je ne dis, ne disais, tu qu'à deux personnes*' (p. 145 of the
French text; 'We tried to say "thou" to each other, but it didn't
work. For my part, I use, or have used, "thou" with only two
people'). One of the two is his son; the other was probably his
wife.

Malone, too, shows in his writings a view of mankind in which
each individual is seen as imprisoned within himself, however he
may attempt to come out of his solitude into society. He says of
Mr and Mrs Saposcat that when they talked together they did

not really communicate; they only pursued separate thoughts on a single theme :

> Starting from a given theme their minds laboured in unison. They had no conversation properly speaking. They made use of the spoken word in much the same way as the guard of a train makes use of his flags, or of his lantern [*Malone*, p. 11].

In another place Malone pictures an entire world of people futilely trying to escape their solitude by clustering together for a few minutes. He describes a city at the end of the afternoon as people leave their places of work and face the long evening ahead of them :

> The doors open and spew them out, each door its contingent. For an instant they cluster in a daze, huddled on the sidewalk or in the gutter, then set off singly on their appointed ways. . . . And God help him who longs, for once, in his recovered freedom, to walk a little way with a fellow-creature, no matter which, unless of course by a merciful chance he stumble on one in the same plight. Then they take a few paces happily side by side, then part . . . [*Malone*, p. 56].

Malone himself, at one time, sought companionship in a similar manner. At first it was with 'an Israelite' named Jackson; then when that relationship failed, he sought the friendship of others, but with no more success :

> My relations with Jackson were of short duration. I could have put up with him as a friend, but unfortunately he found me disgusting, as did Johnson, Wilson, Nicholson and Watson, all whoresons. I then tried, for a space, to lay hold of a kindred spirit among the inferior races, red, yellow, chocolate, and so on. And if the plague-stricken had been less difficult of access I would have intruded on them too, ogling, sidling, leering, in-effing and conating, my heart palpitating. With the insane too I failed, by a hair's-breadth [*Malone*, p. 44].

Now, having given up such hopes, he only feels contemptuous of them, but that he still feels some longing to share his life with someone can be seen from the manner in which he lingers over the word 'home' when, thinking of the couple who live in the house across the way, he says, 'The man has not yet come home. Home' (p. 15). The second 'home' was added in the English translation, probably to emphasize this feeling (the French text, p. 31; had only *'L'homme n'est pas encore rentré'*).

Malone's compulsive story-telling and his concern with possessions, in addition to being the results of a compulsion to mental activity and of a need to bolster his security against irrational anxieties, are also attempts to distract himself from a too intense awareness of his solitude. He says as much about his attachment to his possessions : '. . . but for the company of these little objects . . . I might have been reduced to the society of nice people or to the consolations of some religion or other . . .' (p. 75). And one of the reasons he begins to tell the story of Sapo, whose name later becomes Macmann, is that when his earlier characters deserted him, 'I found myself alone, in the dark' (p. 2).

Into his characters, on the other hand, Malone puts a desire for solitude that may be in part a projection of his own aspirations, a picture of a person as delivered from the need for company as he would himself like to be. Macmann, listing to himself the advantages of living in the House of St John of God, includes in his compilation, along with food and lodging and superb views, the fact that his former sexual partner, Moll, is dead and that there is 'no human contact except with Lemuel, who went out of his way to avoid him' (p. 108). On the few occasions on which Lemuel, his keeper, did not avoid him Macmann felt annoyed at the breach of his solitude.

The sexual lives, or at least the sexual preoccupations, of the characters of the trilogy further illustrate the depth and irrevocability of their isolation. Sexuality, as they understand it, is a purely physical phenomenon, and not a very enjoyable one at that. It offers no serious hope of escape from solitude. Malone says, for example, in the description of the city at the end of the working day when people form momentary groups for company, 'At this hour then erotic craving accounts for the majority of couples' (p. 56). To describe love as erotic craving is to reduce it to merely the satisfaction of separate appetites. The couples are only conjunctions of individuals; when their function is only the satisfaction of erotic cravings, there is no spiritual interpenetration and consequently no escape from separateness.[3] Malone says as much not

long afterward in a description of the man and woman who live
in the house across the way. They are making love one night in
front of their window. The imagery he uses is reminiscent of Book
IV of *De Rerum Natura* in which Lucretius discusses the same sort
of futile attempt by lovers to merge their bodies so as to become
one person. Malone sees them writhing in embrace and can only
surmise that they are trying to compress their two bodies into one :

> For they cleave so fast together that they seem a single body,
> and consequently a single shadow. But when they totter it is
> clear they are twain, and in vain they clasp with the energy of
> despair, it is clear we have here two distinct and separate bodies,
> each enclosed within its own frontiers . . . [*Malone*, p. 65].

Nowhere in the trilogy can carnal love transcend the separateness
of 'two distinct and separate bodies, each enclosed within its own
frontiers.' Nor do the protagonists ever make any but the most
feeble efforts in this direction. Whatever sexual activity there is
is usually between two people so old they can hardly manage it,
or it is simply masturbation, the solitary pleasure *par excellence*.

Moran must at one time have engaged in sexual intercourse with
a woman, since he did manage to produce a son, but he never
says anything about it in his narrative. He never even mentions
an appetite for women, and although he seems to be interested in
masturbation, even that affords him little pleasure : 'I took advantage of being alone at last, with no other witness than God, to
masturbate. My son must have had the same idea, he must have
stopped on the way to masturbate. I hope he enjoyed it more than
I did' (*Molloy*, pp. 198-99).

Molloy's world, unlike Moran's, includes lovers, and Molloy
himself has been one of them, but it is significant also that hetero-
sexual intercourse seems always to have been something less than
pleasant for him and that he too prefers masturbation. As Molloy
describes his intercourse with the old woman whose name he thinks
was Edith or Ruth, it seems more trouble than it was worth :

> She had a hole between her legs, oh not the bunghole I had
> always imagined, but a slit, and in this I put, or rather she put,
> my so-called virile member, not without difficulty, and I toiled
> and moiled until I discharged or gave up trying or was begged

by her to stop. A mug's game in my opinion and tiring on top of that, in the long run [*Molloy*, p. 76].

And he goes on to add that 'twixt finger and thumb tis heaven in comparison' (p. 77).

For the Unnamable, sexual desire does not involve women at all. The only form of sexual behaviour that even seems appealing to him is masturbation, and it must have been a long time since he last did that because he hardly remembers the word for it and is surprised at the idea of still having enough potency left:

The tumefaction of the penis! The penis, well now, that's a nice surprise, I'd forgotten I had one. What a pity I have no arms, there might still be something to be wrung from it. No, tis better thus. At my age, to start manstuprating again, it would be indecent. And fruitless [*Unnamable*, pp. 62-63].

Nor do women figure in the fantasies with which he tries to stimulate his erotic appetites. Rather he gets the best results from thinking of horses' rumps: 'With a yo heave ho, concentrating with all my might on a horse's rump, at the moment when the tail rises, who knows, I might not go altogether empty-handed away' (p. 63).

The only time the Unnamable ever mentions sexual intercourse with a woman is when he expresses his disgust with the family he is supposed to have lost in the story of the one-legged world-traveler. He speaks of intercourse with his wife as only an act of revenge against mankind: '. . . the two cunts . . . the one for ever accursed that ejected me into this world and the other, in-fundibuliform, in which, pumping my likes, I tried to take my revenge' (pp. 48-49).

It is ironic that characters who cannot think of love as anything more than the satisfaction of physical appetites find so little satis-faction even in the physical sense. The one case in the trilogy in which sexual intercourse is seen as offering any pleasure at all, that of the affair between Macmann and Moll, is itself more of a parody of sexuality than a sympathetic description of it. Their common decrepitude renders the whole endeavour grotesque:

There sprang up gradually between them a kind of intimacy which, at a given moment, led them to lie together and copulate as best they could. For given their age and scant experience of carnal love, it was only natural they should not succeed, at the first shot, in giving each other the impression they were made for each other. The spectacle was then offered of Macmann trying to bundle his sex into his partner's like a pillow into a pillow-slip, folding it in two and stuffing it in with his fingers. But far from losing heart they warmed to their work. And though both were completely impotent they finally succeeded, summoning to their aid all the resources of the skin, the mucus and the imagination, in striking from their dry and feeble clips a kind of sombre gratification. So that Moll exclaimed, being (at that stage) the more expansive of the two, Oh would we had but met sixty years ago! But on the long road to this what flutterings, alarms and bashful fumblings, of which only this, that they gave Macmann some insight into the meaning of the expression, Two is company [*Malone*, p. 89].

Although this is the one case in the trilogy in which something like a spiritual union takes place through sexual intercourse, it is a classic example of the exception proving the rule. Whatever union there is between Macmann and Moll is only momentary and of little importance. Moll realizes this. She tells Macmann that it is fortunate they are both almost dead because otherwise they would have time to see through the romantic illusion :

. . . we shall not have time to grow to loathe each other, to see our youth slip by, to recall with nausea the ancient rapture, to seek in the company of third parties, you on the one hand, I on the other, that which together we can no longer compass, in a word to get to know each other [*Malone*, p. 90].

Even the hope that their love might last the brief space between their belated meeting and death proves too sanguine. It is only a short time until Moll dies, and even before this she has grown tired of her 'sweet old hairy Mac.' As Macmann grows fond of her, she loses interest in him. Malone says that the brief moment of equal ardor is not even worth describing :

Of the brief period of plenitude between these two extremes, when between the warming up of the one party and the cooling down of the other there was established a fleeting equality of temperature, no further mention will be made. For if it is indispensable to have in order not to have had and in order to have no longer, there is no obligation to expatiate upon it [*Malone*, pp. 92-93].

The intensity of Macmann's attachment to Moll at the end while she is dying, is rendered ridiculous by her loss of interest in him and by the grotesquerie of 'Macmann's desire to take her, all stinking, yellow, bald and vomiting, in his arms' (p. 94). Sexual union, which in the works of some writers, D. H. Lawrence for example, is the only means of escape from the solitude to which each person is confined by a conscious individual personality, in Beckett's trilogy affords no significant hope.

Since the Unnamable's opportunities for sexual congress are limited to say the least, he employs a different set of images to express the intensity and inevitability of his isolation. The imagery he finds most effective for this is simply a further elaboration of the imagery of hell. One of the important features of the traditional Christian picture of hell was the excruciating solitude of those who had rejected both the love of God and the love of man in favor of total isolation and whose damnation consisted in their free but perpetual and irrevocable affirmation of that choice. According to this tradition, the damned were cut off not only from God, but even from each other, so that even if hell were densely populated, each damned soul would always be alone. The Unnamable, trying to understand his own hell, imagines it at times to be empty except for him : '. . . alone, and mute, lost in the smoke, it is not real smoke, there is no fire, no matter, strange hell that has no heating, no denizens . . .' (*Unnamable*, p. 100). In another place he speculates that perhaps the hell he is in does have denizens, each in eternal isolation carrying on a private monologue, but he concludes that, whether this hypothesis is true or not, the one incontrovertible fact is his own solitude :

. . . perhaps I'm not alone, perhaps a whole people is here, and the voice its voice, coming to me fitfully, we would have lived, been free a moment, now we talk about it, each one to himself, each one out loud for himself, and we listen, a whole people, talking and listening, all together, that would ex, no, I'm alone, perhaps the first, or perhaps the last, talking alone, listening alone, alone alone . . . [*Unnamable*, p. 172]

At one time there crosses his mind what seems to be a faint suspicion that if he is in this state because of a moral failure it may be, as in the case of the Christian hell, the sin of choosing to be alone, the choice of placing himself at the center of the universe. This seems at least to be what is meant when, in thinking about the necessity to talk about himself in order to go silent, he mentions the possibility that his sin may be this very tendency to center all his thoughts on himself : '. . . I'll never be silent, never at peace. Unless I try once more, just once more, one last time, to say what has to be said, about me, I feel it's about me, perhaps that's the mistake I make, perhaps that's my sin . . .' (*Unnamable*, p. 150). This is only a guess on his part, however, and no more is made of it.

What he slowly comes to understand is that the place he is in and the reasons he is in it are completely mysterious. There are only three certainties in his life, the three inescapable realities mentioned earlier : '. . . the inability to speak, the inability to be silent, and solitude. . . .' At the beginning of his volume, when he is still relatively naïve, he thinks it may be possible to alleviate his solitude by telling stories about imaginary characters : 'I shall not be alone in the beginning. I am of course alone. Alone. . . . I shall have company. In the beginning. A few puppets. Then I'll scatter them, to the winds, if I can' (p. 4). By the time he is little more than halfway through the volume, however, it is clear that he cannot scatter them any more than he can claim to have invented them. They seem to control him more than he them. All he will ever be able to know for certain is that he will always be alone and that for him there is no way out of what he calls, on page 130, 'this hell of stories.'

CHAPTER IX

Beyond the Trilogy

'It seems to me I am rather musical this time I have that in my life this time.' *How It Is*

The completion of the trilogy brought Beckett's art to a temporary impasse. In its three volumes he succeeded in explicating fully the themes that the earlier novels had announced but only partially developed. Consequently he was left with no further possibilities to explore in this area. And in *The Unnamable* he brought to its full conclusion a process of simplification and denudation of fiction that had begun as early as *Watt*. During the course of his career as a novelist, Beckett can be seen purifying his fiction of almost all the conventional properties of the traditional realistic novel in order to concentrate on the bare essentials of the human condition. In this process, he has rarefied his art almost to the limit of possibility. In the last volume of the trilogy, he is left with nothing but a disembodied voice repeating itself endlessly. If his career had stopped at this point, it would have seemed that just as Beckett's characters were groping toward silence, so Beckett himself, as an artist, was groping toward a blank page. It must have appeared this way to Beckett, too, for a while, since he said in 1956, speaking of the difficulty he was having in continuing to write fiction :

> Since then [1950] I haven't written anything. Or at least nothing that has seemed to me valid. The French work brought me to the point where I felt I was saying the same thing over and over again. For some authors writing gets easier the more they

write. For me it gets more and more difficult. For me the area of possibilities gets smaller and smaller. . . . In the last book—'L'Innomable'—there's complete disintegration. No 'I,' no 'have,' no 'being.' No nominative, no accusative, no verb. There's no way to go on.

The very last thing I wrote—'Textes pour rien'—was an attempt to get out of the attitude of disintegration, but it failed.[1]

The reason *Textes pour rien (Texts for nothing)*[2] was a failure was that it repeated too simply the themes and style of *The Unnamable*. At first, in 'Text I,' it looks as if Beckett is experimenting with a return to a kind of realism. The narrator is presented as a concrete person in a realistic setting, sitting on the top of a mountain or hill. The mountain itself has realistic details—'Quag, heath up to the knees, faint sheep tracks, troughs scooped deep by the rains' (p. 75)—though the view is obscured by mist so that the narrator has to describe it imaginatively, in interestingly picturesque language : '. . . the distant sea in hammered lead, the so-called golden vale so often sung, the double valleys, the glacial loughs, the city in its haze . . .' (p. 76). He says that if it were a clear day he would be able, with the help of a telescope, to see his home.[3] He speaks of how 'they' had once wanted him to stay at home and how they now want him to return. As he talks about these vague figures, however, he begins to sound once again like the Unnamable talking about his nameless tormentors : '. . . they all have the same voice, the same ideas. . . . They are up above, all round me. . . .'

It is difficult to say whether the series of 'texts' all relate to the same narrator or not. There are thirteen separate texts, with no particularly apparent connection. If they do relate to the same character, they portray his rapid disorientation and disembodiment, which transform him into a vague figure without definite identity, whose being, like that of the Unnamable, seems to derive from a voice speaking through him. The opening of 'Text II'—'Above is the light, the elements . . . the living find their ways . . .' (p. 81)—reminds one of the Unnamable's references to his life above in the island. It also sounds like an anticipation of *How It Is*, the narrator of which talks frequently about a world 'above in the light.'

Thinking of this world above, the narrator goes on to reminisce about various people presumably up there : 'Mr Joly,' the verger of Moran's church; a Mother Calvet; and a Piers, evidently Piers the Plowman, since he is described as 'pricking his oxen o'er the plain' (p. 83). Later 'texts' mention other memories, memories of the narrator's childhood when he was looked after by a nanny, memories of himself and a friend as a couple of war veterans, and so on. Molloy and Malone are mentioned, and Pozzo, from *Waiting for Godot*, is spoken of as having a castle and retainers.

The narrator never manages to proceed very far in developing stories about any of these figures. Much of the time he sounds almost exactly like the Unnamable in the latter half of his volume trying to tell stories but both unable and unwilling to do so. His main attention he gives to the voice and to the problem of escaping from it. He feels that the voice talking through him is not his but an alien force occupying him. Although at the beginning (in 'Text II') he sounds as if he is afraid of running out of words before he can finish his story, he later comes to wish that the voice would leave him so that he could cease to exist. He speaks of Molloy and Malone as fortunate because as mortals—'those mere mortals, happy mortals' (p. 92)—they had the hope of eventually dying. Like the Unnamable again, he speculates occasionally that perhaps the voice wants him to become born as a character in a story before it will let him go silent.

At the end, however, he says that all he has said about the voice and about his relationship to it is both true and not true, that the reality of it all is indescribable, and he closes both hoping and not hoping that someday the voice will terminate in silence.

The title, *Texts for nothing*, is itself significant as an indication of Beckett's aesthetic concerns in his work following the trilogy. As his work has become more and more denuded, with regard to both its style and its material, Beckett has in fact come to feel that 'nothing'—that is, the state of mind of a person who can do nothing and who knows that he can know nothing—is the special area of experience that he is called upon to explore :

> I'm working with impotence, ignorance. I don't think impotence has been exploited in the past. . . . My little exploration is that whole zone of being that has always been set aside by artists as something unuseable—as something by definition incompatible with art.

I think anyone nowadays who pays the slightest attention to his own experience finds it the experience of a non-knower, a non-can-er. . . .[4]

Beckett's fiction since the last volume of the trilogy has been an attempt to find an artistic form which would be in its own way orderly and beautiful, but which would express what life feels like to a person, or perhaps one should say a nonperson, who can know nothing and who can say nothing about the nothing that he knows.

It is undoubtedly also significant for an understanding of Beckett's aesthetic intentions that the phrase 'texte pour rien' is a literary equivalent for the musical term 'mesure pour rien.'[5] A 'mesure pour rien,' in music, is a bar's rest, a period of silence. In naming his work *Textes pour rien* Beckett was suggesting that he was trying to construct a work of art out of brief periods of silence, and in fact he has done something of the sort, since the thirteen texts say virtually nothing: the narrator uses words, but he negates their value by explicitly stating that everything they appear to be saying is false. What is especially significant, however, about the parallel between Beckett's title and the musical term is that a bar's rest in music is a very special sort of silence. It is not just silence in an absolute or simple sense; it is silence as an integral part of a formal structure. Music is something which, in itself, means nothing, but which nevertheless embodies beauty. As Beckett has found himself more and more restricted in his thematic material, he has become increasingly concerned with form, and in his latest novel, *How It Is*, he has produced something which, both in its use of sound and in its over-all structure, is, as I shall show, very close to music.

How It Is[6] is a work which says no more than *Texts for nothing*, but which is more successful because it says its nothing with a very impressive formal perfection. The story is the simplest of any of Beckett's novels. It has to do with the nameless narrator's encounter —whether purely imaginary or in any sense real is not made clear —with another character to whom he gives the name Pim. The indefiniteness of this meeting with Pim is interestingly reminiscent of the similar vagueness of the encounter or nonencounter between the faun and the nymphs in Mallarmé's *L'Après-midi d'un faune*. The similarity is especially interesting in view of the fact that Mallarmé in his own time was as preoccupied as Beckett with the idea of nothingness, with the inadequacy of words, and with the problems of wresting art from silence. It would seem that in *How It Is* Beckett is doing with the novel something very like that which *symbolisme*, at least as represented by Mallarmé, did with verse in the nineteenth century : he is turning his back on realism in order to create a new type of novel which works by means of suggestion and evocation rather than direct statement and which treats thematic content primarily as a vehicle for form. The big difference between Mallarmé and Beckett, of course, lies in the fact that whereas Mallarmé, in his art, tried to turn away from sordid reality, Beckett plunges his characters right into the muck of it.

As far as the unpleasantness of existence is concerned, the narrator of *How It Is* is probably even worse off than the Unnamable was. He is alone in a dark, vast place crawling through an apparently endless swamp of slimy mud. He is dragging with him a sack containing cans of tunny fish. His only other possession is his can opener. The certitudes of his life, as he discusses them at the beginning of his story, are mud, darkness, the sack, the cans, silence, and solitude; and that even these minimal certainties are also uncertain is made clear by the end of the book.

The silence the narrator refers to is, of course, only the silence of the place, not silence within him. Like the Unnamable and like the narrator of *Texts for nothing*, the narrator of *How It Is* is the instrument of a voice speaking through him with which he does not identify : 'scraps of an ancient voice in me not mine' (p. 7). As he describes it, his story is being spoken by the voice, which he repeatedly says he is only quoting : 'here then part one how is was before Pim we follow I quote the natural order more or less my life last state last version what remains bits and scraps I hear it' (p. 7).

The story he tells is in three parts : before Pim, with Pim, and after Pim. The 'before Pim' part is an exposition of the basic situation as described in the paragraph above. His many references to a life above in the light would seem to indicate that he has since died and is now in another world which receives people after death. He frequently compares the place he is in to the traditional hell. When he wonders at one point, for example, if perhaps he might meet a llama or an alpaca somewhere in the mud, he dismisses the idea with the same argument that Christian theology has traditionally used against the idea of an afterlife for animals : 'no a beast here no the soul is de rigueur the mind too a minimum of each otherwise too great an honour' (p. 14). Speaking in another place of his desire to sleep he compares his own undeserving state to that of the souls in torment he says he used to pray for, presumably in his life above in the light :

> prayer in vain to sleep I have no right to it yet I haven't yet deserved it prayer for prayer's sake when all fails when I think of the souls in torment true torment true souls who have no right to it no right ever to sleep we're talking of sleep I prayed for them once . . . [p. 36].

And not long after this, he says explicitly that he is 'in outer hell' (p. 43).

The place he is in does seem hellish enough, but the reason he uses the image of hell to describe it is primarily that this was the language he was taught in the other life. He can remember his mother sitting on a veranda teaching him the fundamentals of Christian religion : 'on my knees whelmed in a nightshirt I pray according to her instructions that's not all she closes her eyes and drones a snatch of the so-called Apostles' Creed' (pp. 15-16). As was the case in *The Unnamable*, the comparison to the Christian hell is only an analogy, but it is the only analogy available that seems even remotely adequate.

During the first part, before Pim, the narrator also has various other memories or fleeting visions besides that of his mother. Nothing much ever develops from any of these except in one case, a three-page long fantasy in which he imagines he meets a girl under a blue sky in April or May and walks in the country with her and her dog. Most of his time in the first part he spends anticipating the meeting with Pim. In fact he so frequently reverts to this subject that he has to keep reminding himself that he is not to talk of that until the second part. It looks almost as if in his loneliness he is so eager to get to the encounter that he has to make an effort not to rush ahead in his story. The first part ends with a description of his surprise when, crawling through the mud in the absolute darkness, he suddenly comes across another person :

semi-side right left leg left arm push pull flat on the face mute
imprecations scrabble in the mud every half-yard . . . the hand
dips clawing for the take instead of the familiar slime an arse
two cries one mute end of part one before Pim that's how it
was before Pim [p. 48].

Although the meeting with Pim does involve a kind of contact and
communication, the nature of this contact is such that it only
serves to emphasize the isolation of the narrator. In part one he
spoke of the relief it would be for him to have company in his
solitude—'a procession what comfort in adversity others what
comfort' (p. 48)—but the relationship he comes to have with Pim is
hardly what one would normally call company; it is the relationship
of a tormentor with his victim. Instead of treating Pim as a person,
the narrator treats him as an object, just another one of his
possessions. In fact, the first meeting with Pim is described as a
kind of taking possession of him : 'my hand recoils hangs a moment
it's vague in mid air then slowly sinks again and settles firm and
even with a touch of ownership already on the miraculous flesh'
(p. 51).

It is 'miraculous flesh,' not because there is anything sacred
to him about human personality, but because the fact that this
new possession has living flesh makes it capable of offering him
greater possibilities of amusement than could his sack, his tins, or
his can opener. Flesh can be tortured, and to torture it is the first
thing that occurs to the narrator, to 'claw dig deep furrows drink
the screams' (p. 53).

For a while, before the torment begins, the two lie there together
in the mud, and the narrator says that these were 'good moments'
(p. 54), but the best moments—'the best in my life perhaps'—
were those of the next phase of their relationship, the training
period. In this period take place the 'bud and bloom of relations
proper' (p. 57) as the narrator teaches Pim a language of knocks
and jabs :

table of basic stimuli one sing nails in armpit two speak blade
in arse three stop thump on skull four louder pestle on kidney
five softer index in anus six bravo clap athwart arse seven lousy
same as three eight encore same as one or two as may be [p. 69].

Needless to say, by the time Pim is well trained his anus and his armpit are both gaping wounds.

After this the narrator says he made Pim tell him about his life above in the light. Actually, it is difficult to believe that the stories that follow are really those of Pim. Since the narrator says at several times during the book that Pim himself was only imaginary—'never any Pim never was never anything of all this' (p. 98)—the stories would seem more likely to be those of the narrator's own previous life, assuming he really had one, or else just more fantasies.

Whomever the stories refer to—and it really is not very important since human experience, for *How It Is* as for other Beckett novels, tends always to be the same—they describe a life that, although it took place above among people, was just as solitary as the present life in the mud. The speaker tells of how he 'never knew anyone always ran fled' (p. 78). The descriptions of the speaker's father and of his mother, very like the mother of the narrator as described in part one, are extremely brief and do not show any particular affection. The only extended story is that of the speaker's wife, a Pam Prim, who apparently committed suicide. No reason is given for her suicide, but it would seem very likely to have been from the loneliness of being married to a person as solitary as the speaker. Their marital relationship, as it is described, does not seem to have offered much to either : 'Pam Prim we made love every day then every third then the Saturday then just the odd time to get rid of it tried to revive it through the arse too late she fell from the window or jumped . . .' (p. 77). As the speaker tells the story, he comments wryly that just as he never loved her in the life above, so now when he recalls her his attention is less on her than on the objects around her in the vision : 'iron bed glossy white two foot wide all was white high off the ground vision of love in it see others' furniture and not the loved one' (p. 77).

If it really is Pim speaking in this story, then he and the narrator are very much alike, since the narrator, too, is more concerned with things than with people. Although he asks Pim repeatedly, 'DO YOU LOVE ME?' by writing the letters out in majuscules on Pim's back, he is really much fonder of Pim's sack than he is of Pim : 'I let go the sack let go Pim that's the worst letting go the sack' (p. 75). He does not know why sacks should mean so much to him, but it is obvious that he cherishes them with an intense passion :

> . . . this sack I always said so this sack for us here is something more than a larder than a pillow for the head than a friend to turn to a thing to embrace a surface to cover with kisses something far more we don't profit by it in any way any more and we cling to it . . . [p. 66].

When he and Pim began the third phase of their relationship, that of the stories, one of the first things he did was take away Pim's sack, even though Pim clung to it desperately : 'first take away his sack he resists I claw his left hand to the bone . . . the blood he must have lost' (p. 65). At the end of part two, as Pim crawls away leaving his sack behind, the narrator is left to the self-centered isolation that has always been his real desire : 'myself alone at last no more Pim me alone in the dark the mud (p. 99).

Part three is devoted mainly to the narrator's speculations about the place he is in and his situation in it. Returned again to total solitude, he becomes a prey to a need to know similar to that we have seen in all of Beckett's previous characters. In this case, however, there is an important difference. Compared with the Unnamable's desperate, anguished struggle to understand, the speculations of the narrator of this book seem almost like a game.

He begins with the speculation that long ago in 'the vast past . . . the extreme old' (p. 103), in the period before that recounted in part one, he was visited by a Bem as he himself had visited Pim and that eventually a Bom will come to him as Bem had. Much of what follows is a series of variations on this theme. He examines the possibility that there might be a million people in this place, and he composes an elaborate diagram of the paths these people might follow in order to come together at regular intervals into half a million couples. Whether there are three, four, or a million, however, each of them he says, will always be fundamentally alone since their relations will always be those of tormentor and victim, 'always two strangers uniting in the interests of torment' (p. 121). All they can give to each other is the satisfaction a tormentor receives from the screams of his victim : 'one drinks one gives to drink' (p. 122).

The most interesting aspect of these speculations of the narrator is their elaborate symmetry. When he imagines a half million couples, he imagines them coming together and parting simultaneously and then coming together again in such a way that each of the tormentors and victims will alternate roles every other encounter. And each victim leaves his sack with his tormentor and receives one in turn from his next victim : 'Pim left me without his sack he left his sack with me I left my sack with Bem I'll leave my sack with Bom I left Bem without my sack to go towards Pim' (p. 111). Of course this last matter damages the symmetry of the pattern, as the narrator realizes, since it fails to account for the fact that as he was moving toward Pim in part one he had a sack. If he left his sack with Bem, then how did he come to have one on the road to Pim? He attempts to account for this by supposing that each of the travelers somehow picks up a sack on his travels at some point :

> number 777777 leaves number 777776 on his way unwitting towards number 777778 finds the sack without which he would not go far takes it unto himself and continues on his way the same to be taken by number 777776 in his turn and after him by number 777775 and so back to the unimaginable number 1 each one no sooner on his way than he finds the sack indispensable to his journey [p. 136].

This hypothesis leads in turn to another problem, the problem of how the sacks happen to be in the right places so that they will be able to pick them up as they set out on their journeys. The narrator attempts to deal with this issue by positing the existence of a supreme power, 'a love who all along the track at the right places according as we need them deposits our sacks' (p. 138).

In his speculations about the nature of this being who provides the sacks, he goes on, like so many Beckett characters before him, to assimilate him to the traditional God of Christianity : 'to whom given our number not unreasonable to attribute exceptional powers or else at his beck assistants innumerable.' This interpretation seems particularly felicitous to the narrator because it will allow him, in pursuance of the principle of parsimony,' to improve his hypothetical model of his world aesthetically by eliminating from it a Kram and Krim, about whom he had previously speculated at length. He had needed Kram and Krim as witness and scribe, respectively, to his life in the mud. The hypothesis of a God, or godlike being, who can serve as witness as well as fill numerous other functions, enables the narrator to simplify his model, rendering it more orderly and thereby more beautiful.

Throughout the book, the narrator's repeated comments—'something wrong there'—on the manner in which he is composing his story shows that he is less a person like the Unnamable trying to wrest meaning from the absurd than an artist concerned principally with building a satisfying formal structure. His speculations are consciously literary, and although they probably still involve a certain amount of the old frustrating desire to understand the meaningless that drove Beckett's other characters to endless puzzling, their purpose in this case seems to be primarily that of a game, a kind of artistic playfulness, with which to pass the time. At the end he acknowledges that this 'exquisitely organized' (p. 143) world is really only a construction of his own imagination : 'all these calculations yes explanations yes the whole story from beginning to end yes completely false' (p. 144).

The reason the narrator of *How It Is* needs to play with formal patterns in order to pass the time is that his time, like that of the Unnamable, is not the sort that passes of its own accord. Time, in his world, is always the same because it endlessly repeats itself : 'this old life same old words same old scraps millions of times each time the first . . . scraps of an antique rigmarole immemorial imperishable' (pp. 133-34). He feels that the most adequate way to speak of time is by means of spatial metaphors, such as 'vast tracts of time' (*'un temps énorme'*), a phrase he repeats over and over. Time does not seem to him to move in any way at all; rather it seems a sort of vast, formless space in which, as he says at the end of the book after denying the whole story of crawling, encounters, and sacks, he only lies in the mud eternally fixed in one spot : 'flat on my belly yes in the mud yes the dark yes' (p. 146).

It is the formlessness of this kind of time that makes it especially unpleasant. The need to know that we have seen in so many of Beckett's characters is to a large extent merely a need to impose some kind of form on experience, and even when knowledge as such seems a lost cause, the need for form persists. At the very beginning of the book the narrator speaks of his futile efforts to ascribe form to time. The use of language referring to seasons,

F

days, and years, he says, belongs to the other world above in the light, not to his world : 'these words of those for whom and under whom and all about the earth turns and all turns these words here again days nights years seasons that family' (p. 17). He continues to use the old language only because he knows now that it would be hopeless to try to find new words to fit his present condition : 'no searching not even for a language meet for me meet for here no more searching.' Once, he says, he derived a certain satisfaction from the ticking of Pim's watch (p. 58), evidently because the ticks seemed to be measuring and thereby giving a kind of shape to time, but in the present he understands the futility of this : 'to have Pim's timepiece . . . and nothing to time' (p. 40).

The narrator is too clear-sighted to be able to deceive himself. He knows that the only reality is chaos. Since, however, his mind, like all human minds, is such that it cannot rest in chaos, his final solution is to impose a form on his experience arbitrarily by making up a story. By this means he will be able, he says, to 'divide into three a single eternity' (p. 24). Although he will have to use the old words to say 'the same things'—that is, he will have to explore again the old themes of isolation, the need to know, the need to keep going, the desire to end, and so on—the formal pattern of the story is within his control. It is a small measure of freedom, but the use he puts it to is impressive.

The composition he creates with his freedom is, both in its larger structure and in its combinations of individual words, something very close to music.

Unfortunately, the English translation is not always adequate to convey the musical effect that can be found in a number of frequently repeated phrases in the original French. A good example is the phrase *'quelque chose là qui ne va pas,'* which recurs constantly throughout the book. The French has a rhythmic quality, together with alliteration and assonance, none of which have any equivalent in the English version's relatively flat sounding 'something wrong there.' Another example is a phrase that is very important to part two of the book and which is repeated several times in the early pages of that section : *'un bon moment ce sont des bons moments'* (French text, p. 68, for example). The English translation, 'a good moment they are good moments' (p. 54), lacks the resonant nasal *'on'* sound which gives this phrase its special ring. A similar assonance based on the sound, *'en,'* occurs in the recurrent '*de temps en temps*' of the French text, which becomes in English simply 'now and then.'

The musical structure of the book as a whole, however, is equally clear in both texts. This involves a compositional pattern very similar to that which in music would be called sonata form. Sonata form consists of three parts, exposition, development, and recapitulation, usually ending with a coda. The parts of *How It Is* correspond fairly closely to these. The important difference between this work and a typical work in traditional sonata form is that whereas the musical form traditionally begins with a certain harmony, modulates in the development section into other keys which sound discordant in relation to the original tonic key, and finally resolves this tension with a return to the tonic in the third section, *How It Is* begins in a mood of depression with a chaos which is experienced as discordant, modulates in the central section into a rather more cheerful, harmonious mood, and then returns to chaos. The traditional principle of tonal music is the resolution of discord in harmony. Beckett uses the same principle in *How It Is*, only he reverses the order of precedence. Tonal music establishes harmony as the fundamental reality, representing discord as a more or less powerful, but not invincible, threat. In *How It Is* the fundamental reality is chaos.

As in the exposition section of sonata form, part one of *How It Is* sets forth the basic themes of the piece. The trilogy had taken essentially the same themes and explored them at length, trying to reveal as fully as possible their cognitive content. In *How It Is* the emphasis is no longer on the cognitive content of the themes. They are not explored in a systematic way for the sake of the information they have to offer about human nature and the nature of the universe. Rather they appear as brief fragments, 'scraps of an ancient voice' (p. 7), and they are used not for their intrinsic interest but as compositional elements in a formal structure.

The principal themes presented in part one are: the voice and the problem of the narrator's relation to it; possessions and his irrational attachment to them; the need to go on; the desire to end; solitude; Pim; the life above in the light, primarily represented by memories of his mother and the Christian religion; the fantasy of the walk with the girl and her dog; and the possibility that there are witnesses observing him. In some cases these themes are almost melodic. For example, when the narrator describes the scene in which he is a child with his mother, the sound itself is lyrical : 'we are on a veranda smothered in verbena the scented sun dapples the red tiles yes' (p. 15). Or when he thinks of the life above in the light as a state offering the possibility of escape from his present misery : 'above if I were above the stars already and from the belfreys the brief hour' (p. 43). The melodious quality of this last passage is even more evident in the sound of the original French : *'là-haut si j'étais là-haut les étoiles déja et aux beffrois l'heure brève'* (French text, p. 53). Here the assonance of the repeated *'au'* and *'oi'* sounds in the French compose a kind of verbal music. These lyrical passages, however, are isolated and brief. The basic tone of the first part is one of depression alleviated only by short fantasies or by anticipations of part two.

The second section of sonata form in music develops the thematic material introduced in the first section and modulates it by transposing it into keys often far removed from the main key. The basic function of the development section is to contrast with the two very similar sections that frame it. In *How It Is* the principle development is that of the Pim theme, which was mentioned only briefly and in a fragmentary manner in the first part, but which in the second part takes on clear shape and occupies the center of attention. The other themes carried over from the exposition go through variations related to the Pim theme. The solitude theme and the possessions theme, for example, combine as solitude modulates into a new kind of solitude-in-spite-of-company, and possessions, such as sacks or Pim's watch, become bones of contention separating the two characters. The story of Pam Prim, ostensibly Pim's wife, is a variation on the themes of solitude and the life above in the light. Even Pim's song, the one that he sings when jabbed in the armpit, is built of fragments of motifs from part one : 'he continues the same air . . . a word or two eyes skies the or thee' (p. 64). The eyes in Pim's song are reminiscent of the eyes of the narrator's mother in part one, and the skies recall those of the landscape described in connection with the fantasy of the girl and her dog. The eye motif recurs in the story of Pam Prim : 'the flowers I held them at arm's length before her eyes the things you see right hand left hand before her eyes that was my visit and she forgiving' (p. 77). Here they seem to be associated with feelings of guilt, which are probably the narrator's, since the story of Pim, who is ostensibly the one telling about Pam Prim, is supposed to be the narrator's own fabrication. The idea of guilt, of course, is connected with the theme of solitude, since the fault Pam Prim is forgiving is evidently that of having left her to such solitude that she would want to commit suicide.

The tonal modulation of part two of *How It Is* is more abrupt than that usually found in the development section of musical sonata form. Instead of transposing keys gradually to lead further and further away from the tonic, the 'with Pim' section opens immediately with a tone of relief and pleasure in being delivered from total isolation by the discovery of Pim in the mud. This change of mood is emphasized by the repeated use in the early pages of part two of the phrase, 'they are good moments,' practically the only favorable thing the narrator ever has to say about his situation. As the section moves on—through the guilt feelings associated with Pam Prim, for example, and through the realization that there is no real love between the narrator and Pim—there is a breakdown of this feeling of harmony, eventually leading back to the original discordant feelings of loneliness and despair.

Although there is some further development of thematic material in part three of *How It Is*—such as speculations about the future Bom and his antecedent, Bem, about Kram and Krim, and about the godlike being who provides the sacks—it is essentially a recapitulation of the first section. The story has led the narrator from solitude, through a kind of company, then back again to solitude. As in sonata form, however, the recapitulation is not a simple repetition. In the musical form, the restatement of the exposition usually involves some modification of the key scheme. Something similar happens in *How It Is*. The two solitudes that frame the 'with Pim' section are different in mood because the first was the solitude of a person journeying toward another, while the second is that of the same person abandoned by the other. The narrator, very much the conscious composer, gives this as his reason for constructing the story in this tripartite form instead of having it end with a fourth part about the future Bom :

. . . it is loath for the episode couple even in its twofold aspect to figure twice in the same communication

. . . . . .

loathing most understandable if it be kindly considered that the two solitudes that of the journey and that of the abandon differ appreciably and consequently merit separate treatment whereas the two couples that in which I figure in the north as tormentor and that in which I figure in the south as victim compose the same spectacle exactly [p. 131].

What he is saying is, in effect, that he has chosen to compose his story in the equivalent of sonata form because this form combines the advantages of symmetry and diversity. It is less precisely symmetrical, but more interesting, than simple four-part form would be. Musical composers, also, have generally felt the same way, using four-part form rather seldom and then usually only for a single movement.

The speculations about the simultaneous trajectories of the million inhabitants of the place and about Kram, Krim, Bem, Bom, and the being who provides the sacks, elaborately symmetrical though they are, are really only self-conscious and increasingly desperate efforts to defend form against chaos. By the conclusion of part three, at the end of the coda, the attempts at harmony break down completely, leaving chaos triumphant.

The coda in music can vary greatly in length and importance, but its main purpose is always the same : to heighten the impression of finality. In the case of *How It Is*, there is a kind of coda beginning approximately at the bottom of page 132, immediately following the discussion of the narrator's principles of composition. It proceeds through a rapid summary of the major themes of the book—Bom, the voice, Kram and Krim, the number of voyagers and the relations among them, the sacks, the being in charge of the sacks, communication between tormentor and victim, and the necessity to keep going—to a final rejection of them all : 'the whole story from beginning to end . . . completely false' (p. 144). The last three pages of the book are a climactic crescendo. To suggest increase in intensity, Beckett—or one could with equal appropriateness say the narrator—combines the use of majuscules, to indicate greater volume, with a steady speeding up of the tempo. This acceleration in tempo is achieved by the use of shorter and shorter phrases separated from one another by increasingly frequent repetitions of the monosyllables 'yes,' 'no,' or 'good.' How this works can be seen clearly in these three paragraphs, or versets, from the next to the last page :

and this business of a procession no answer this business of a
procession yes never any procession no nor any journey no never
any Pim no nor any Bom no never anyone no only me no answer
only me yes so that was true yes it was true about me yes and
what's my name no answer WHAT'S MY NAME screams good
only me in any case yes alone yes in the mud yes the dark yes
that holds yes the mud and the dark hold yes nothing to regret
there no with my sack no I beg your pardon no no sack either
no not even a sack with me no

only me yes alone yes with my voice yes my murmur yes when
the panting stops yes all that holds yes panting yes worse and
worse no answer WORSE AND WORSE yes flat on my belly
yes in the mud yes the dark yes nothing to emend there no
the arms spread yes like a cross no answer LIKE A CROSS no
answer YES OR NO yes [pp. 145-46].

In the French text—though unfortunately the same effect could
not be reproduced in the English version—even the sounds of the
words contribute to the feeling of finality in this concluding
crescendo. Take for example, the last lines of the next to the last
paragraph of the book :

. . . *plus troubler le silence pas de réponse crever pas de réponse
CREVER hurlements JE POURRAIS CREVER hurlements JE
VAIS CREVER hurlements bon* [French text, p. 177].

. . . trouble the peace no more no answer the silence no answer
die no answer DIE screams I MAY DIE screams I SHALL
DIE screams good [English text, p. 147].

The explosive '*cre*' sound contrasts with the smoother, more pleasant
nasal '*on*' and '*en*' sounds which precede and follow it. The use of
the nasal at the beginning of the series in '*silence*' and '*réponse*'
establishes the nasal quality as a kind of tonic note. In the concluding '*CREVER hurlements bon*' there is a progression from the
contrasting tone of '*CREVER*' through '*hurlements*,' which contains
the nasal sound dampened somewhat in the '*en*' form, to the
clear enunciation of the rounder '*on*' in the word '*bon*.' This is a
verbal approximation of the traditional musical conclusion which

progresses from dominant through subtonic to tonic.

This is, of course, a harmonic progression, which gives the feeling of moving from discord to harmony. As such, it contrasts with the general triumph of chaos at the end of the book. This is undoubtedly the intention of both Beckett and the narrator. In a universe that is absurd, the only relief from chaos is in aesthetic form. If he is honest, the artist must acknowledge the reality of chaos. His problem is to do this while at the same time retaining control of the form in which he expresses this vision. In *How It Is*, the artist is both completely honest and firmly in control to the very end.

In 1961 in the interview with Tom Driver, Beckett spoke of the problem of the relationship between form and chaos in art as the major challenge confronting twentieth-century writers:

> The confusion . . . is all around us and our only chance now is to let it in. The only chance of renovation is to open our eyes and see the mess.

> .   .   .   .   .   .

> What I am saying does not mean that there will henceforth be no form in art. It only means that there will be new form, and that this form will be of such a type that it admits the chaos and does not try to say that the chaos is really something else. The form and the chaos remain separate. The latter is not reduced to the former. That is why the form itself becomes a preoccupation, because it exists as a problem separate from the material it accommodates. To find a form that accommodates the mess, that is the task of the artist now.[7]

All of Beckett's novels attempt with an impressive artistry and honesty to meet precisely this challenge, to find forms to convey a vision of chaos. In Beckett's writings, the 'mess' is always represented as the basic reality. Any attempts to falsify it are on the part of the characters rather than on the part of the author. The orderliness of *Murphy's* world was read into it by Murphy. *Watt, Molloy,* and *Malone Dies* showed the progressive disorientation of a number of characters as they became disillusioned with the kind of order Murphy was still able to believe in. *The Unnamable* presented the vision of chaos in an almost painfully straightforward way, and in the process it seemed at times to be losing its grasp on form.

How It Is expresses essentially the same vision with surer control, while at the same time it makes important steps forward in exploring the ways in which pure forms like those used in the other arts can be adapted to literary ends. If Beckett writes additional novels, it would seem likely that he will continue to experiment in this area. And even if he writes no further novels, his achievement is already great. Few artists would pose for themselves tasks of the magnitude of those that Beckett has taken on, and still fewer would have the skill and the dedication to fulfill them so successfully.

CHAPTER X

Postscript: Beckett's Fiction since 1964

Beckett has continued to be interested in formal experiment in the novel. Since he did the translation of *How It Is* in 1964 he has published four pieces of short fiction, several of which are reported to be fragments of abandoned novels. 'Imagination morte imaginez' (1965), 'Assez' (1966), and 'Bing' (1966)[1] are short pieces in French which have been translated by the author as 'Imagination Dead Imagine,'[2] 'Enough,'[3] and 'Ping,'[4] respectively. According to the publisher's preface to the British collection, *No's Knife*, where all three appear under the heading 'residua,' 'Ping' is the sole remaining fragment of a novel begun in late 1965. The same note also says that 'Imagination Dead Imagine' is the residue of a longer work. The fourth piece is 'Dans le cylindre' (1967),[5] as yet untranslated.

From the fact that he has begun and abandoned perhaps as many as three novels (the diversity of the residua would seem to preclude a common origin), it appears that Beckett would like to write another novel but is having some difficulty finding a new voice and new themes that will not simply duplicate *The Unnamable* and *How It Is*. 'Imagination Dead Imagine,' which is about the efforts of a failing imagination to keep operating, tends to sound like more of the imagined stories the immediately preceding protagonists either amused themselves with or were afflicted with. 'Enough' consists of the reflections of a now-old man who was just dismissed as a companion by a far older one who had taken him in hand (but with gloves, since he didn't like the feel of another person's skin next to his) when he was a six-year-old child. The two had wandered around the earth a few times together. This story tends toward a more straightforward kind of narrative than the other two because at least there is a sequence of events to describe, but what it would have become if continued is hard to imagine since the events are all in the past. The narrator could perhaps proceed on excursions of his own, which would seem something of a throwback to Molloy and Macmann, or he could ruminate, but Beckett's last two novels already seem to have pretty thoroughly exploited the possibilities of rumination. 'Dans le cylindre,' the shortest of these pieces, is a description of a person in a cylinder.

The most interesting, I believe, of the fragments is 'Ping.' In its very brief space (about one thousand words) it gives a concise, and in its way a strikingly beautiful, picture of a state of mind approaching total silence. Ping, the person being described, is an old man with long white hair standing in an all-white cubicle ('white walls one yard by two white ceiling one square yard'), his eyes fixed forward on the wall in front of him. His distinguishing marks are faded to whiteness. His eyes are 'only just light blue almost white.' As he looks at the wall his mind is almost as blank as everything else; only occasionally a memory of another life ('ping of old') breaks momentarily into his consciousness like a distant 'flash of time.' These flashes bring fragmentary glimpses of a freer world 'blue and white in the wind.' As they come he grasps at them in quest of 'only just perhaps a meaning a nature.' But they are there for a second only, then gone, and Ping remains in the silence, his eyes half closed, 'long lashes imploring.'

The beauty of this piece lies in its tight formal control and in the poignant contrast between, on the one hand, the stark simplicity both of the cubicle and of the language describing it and, on the other, the sudden lyrical surge of the flashes of vision. For a fragment of a longer work it has a remarkable feeling of totality. One could not ask for more, and more would probably only dissipate the power of its concentrated impact. Perhaps Beckett, realizing this, decided that in this case his material was more suited to what is in effect a short prose poem than to a novel.

An eventual further novel, however, is still a definite possibility. Several of his other novels have been preceded by pieces of short fiction similar to those described here. 'The Expelled,' 'The Calmative,' and 'The End,' after all, were a kind of preparation for the trilogy, and *How It Is* seems to contain material that was worked

on but dropped in the 1957 fragment, 'From an Abandoned Work.'[6]
Time and the creative imagination work together, and what they
will produce, only time can show.

NOTES

PREFACE

[1]'How How It Is Was,' *New Yorker*, XL (December 19, 1964), 166.

CHAPTER I

[1]See, for example, Kenneth Alsop, *The Angry Decade* (London: Peter Owen, 1958), p. 38. That this is still a persistent belief among many people can be seen from the fact that it has been repeated even as late as 1967 in *Harper's Bazaar*, No. 3067 (June, 1967), p. 120.

[2]Richard Ellmann, *James Joyce* (New York: Oxford University Press, 1959), p. 662.

[3]Marguerite Guggenheim, *Out of This Century* (New York: Dial Press, 1946), p. 199.

[4]Ellmann, *James Joyce*, p. 661.

[5]See Kenneth Alsop, *The Angry Decade*, p. 37, and Melvin J. Friedman, 'The Novels of Samuel Beckett: An Amalgam of Joyce and Proust,' *Comparative Literature*, XII (Winter, 1960), 47-58.

[6]'Dante . . . Bruno. Vico . . Joyce,' *Our Exagmination Round His Factification for Incamination of Work in Progress* (Paris: Shakespeare and Co., 1929), p. 14.

[7]Tom F. Driver, 'Beckett by the Madeleine,' *Columbia University Forum*, IV (Spring, 1961), 23.

[8]*Ibid.*

[9]*More Pricks than Kicks* (London: Chatto and Windus, 1934), p. 7.

[10]Though two of the stories from this volume have been reprinted: 'Yellow,' in *New World Writing*, No. 10 (New York: Mentor, 1956), and 'Dante and the Lobster,' in *Evergreen Review*, Vol. I, No. 1 (1957).

[11]Though not published until 1953, in Paris.

[12]See Ruby Cohn, '*Watt* in the Light of *The Castle*,' *Comparative Literature*, XIII (Spring, 1961), 154-66. See also John Fletcher, *The Novels of Samuel Beckett* (London: Chatto and Windus, 1964), pp. 88-89.

[13]The volumes of the trilogy originally appeared as *Molloy* (Paris, 1951), *Malone meurt* (Paris, 1951), and *L'Innomable* (Paris, 1953), all published by Éditions de Minuit. The English translations are *Molloy* (New York, 1955), *Malone Dies* (New York, 1956), and *The Unnamable* (New York, 1958). All translations are by Samuel Beckett himself except in the

case of *Molloy*, which he translated in collaboration with Patrick Bowles. All page references, unless otherwise indicated, are to the New York editions published by Grove Press.

[14]See William York Tindall, *Samuel Beckett* (New York and London: Columbia University Press, 1964), pp. 35-36.

[15]Frederick J. Hoffman, *Samuel Beckett: The Language of Self* (Carbondale: Southern Illinois University Press, 1962), pp. 3-55.

[16]Probably the first critic to suggest this was Georges Bataille in 'Le Silence de Molloy,' *Critique*, VII (May 15, 1951), 389.

[17]Niklaus Gessner, *Die Unzulänglichkeit der Sprache: Eine Untersuchung über Formzerfall und Beziehungslosigkeit bei Samuel Beckett* (Zurich: Juris Verlag, 1957), p. 32n., quoted in Ruby Cohn, *Samuel Beckett: The Comic Gamut* (New Brunswick, N.J.: Rutgers University Press, 1962), p. 95.

[18]For an excellent discussion of this subject see Fletcher, *The Novels of Samuel Beckett*, pp. 91-93.

[19]Israel Shenker, 'Moody Man of Letters,' New York *Times*, CV (May 6, 1956), Sec. 2, p. 1.

[20]Driver, 'Beckett by the Madeleine,' p. 23.

CHAPTER II

[1]Page references to *Watt* are to the Grove Press edition, published in New York in 1959.

[2]See Descartes, *Meditationes de Prima Philosophia*, Meditation VI, in *Oeuvres de Descartes*, IX, ed. Adam and Tannery (Paris: Leopold Cerf; 1904), 57-72.

[3]Molloy, for example, refers to 'old Geulincx, dead young, who left me free, on the black boat of Ulysses, to crawl towards the East, along the deck' (*Molloy*, p. 68). Ruby Cohn has pointed out that this is an allusion to a passage from Geulincx's *Ethics*: see her article, 'Philosophical Fragments in the Works of Samuel Beckett,' *Criticism*, VI (Winter, 1964), 36. The narrator of Beckett's story 'The End,' in *Stories and Texts for nothing* (New York: Grove Press, 1967), p. 63, says that he was once given a copy of the *Ethics* of Geulincx, but he does not mention having read it. The narrator of *How It Is* (New York: Grove Press, 1964) mentions Malebranche on page 30.

[4]First published in London in 1931, later reprinted with the same pagination by Grove Press (New York, 1957).

[5]Marcel Proust, *A la recherche du temps perdu* (Paris: Gallimard, 1954), I, 382.

[6]Published in *Transition*, Nos. 16-17 (June, 1929), pp. 268-71. Since this piece is only three pages long, I will give no page references for quotations.

[7]Although *More Pricks Than Kicks* has been out of print since the London, 1934, edition, microfilm copies of this are available in some libraries, and consequently I am giving page references to this edition.

[8]See Fletcher, *The Novels of Samuel Beckett*, pp. 14-16.

[9]Guggenheim, *Out of This Century*, p. 197.

CHAPTER III

[1]*Murphy* was first published in London in 1938. The Grove Press

edition (New York, 1957) has the same pagination.

²This and all subsequent references to Dante are to *La Divina Commedia*, ed. Natalino Sapegno (Milan and Naples: Riccardo Ricciardi, 1957). Translations are my own.

³See Raymond Federman, *Journey to Chaos: Samuel Beckett's Early Fiction* (Berkeley and Los Angeles: University of California Press, 1965), p. 71.

CHAPTER IV

¹The reference to Watt's having once known the stars 'familiarly by name, when dying in London' (p. 212) reminds one of Murphy and suggests that either he is a kind of fictional re-embodiment of Murphy or he once passed through a period in which he lived a life similar to Murphy's and shared some of Murphy's concerns. If he ever did, like Murphy, once seek understanding of the universe and human life in the study of astrology, he has, nevertheless, passed beyond this naïve stage of his quest by the time he begins his journey to Knott's house.

²This is the opening sentence of Aristotle's *Metaphysics*.

³See Tindall, *Samuel Beckett*, p. 20.

⁴There is an interesting similarity here between Watt and Sartre's Antoine Roquentin in *La Nausée* (Paris: Gallimard, 1938), who tries to exorcise a tram seat in Bouville by pinning the name 'tram seat' on it: '*Je murmure: c'est une banquette, un peu comme un exorcisme. Mais le mot reste sur mes lèvres: il refuse d'aller se poser sur la chose*' (p. 159). It would seem very likely that Beckett would have read Sartre by the time he was writing *Watt* in the early 1940's.

⁵John Fletcher, *The Novels of Samuel Beckett*, pp. 91-99, has an excellent discussion of the evolution of Beckett's French style.

⁶There is a typescript of 'Mercier et Camier' in the special collections library of the University of California at Santa Barbara. Raymond Federman, *Journey to Chaos*, pp. 135-76, has an extended discussion of this work. Some excerpts from 'Mercier et Camier' were published as 'Madden and The Umbrella,' translated by Hugh Kenner and Raymond Federman, *Spectrum*, IV, No. 1 (Winter, 1960), 3-11.

⁷See Fletcher, *The Novels of Samuel Beckett*, p. 91.

⁸First published in *Les Temps Modernes*, No. 1 (July, 1946), pp. 107-19. 'La Fin' is a revised version.

⁹New York: Grove Press, 1967. Page references in the text are to this edition. 'La Fin' was translated as 'The End' by Richard Seaver in collaboration with Samuel Beckett. The translation first appeared in *Merlin*, II, No. 3 (Summer-Autumn, 1954), 144-59. It was published again in a revised version in *Evergreen Review*, IV, No. 15 (November-December, 1960), 22-41. 'L'Expulsé' was translated as 'The Expelled' also by Richard Seaver in collaboration with Samuel Beckett and first appeared in *Evergreen Review*, VI, No. 22 (January-February, 1962), 8-20. 'The Calmative' was translated by Beckett alone.

¹⁰See Federman, *Journey to Chaos*, p. 136.

CHAPTER V

¹The travelers are called A and B in the original French text of *Molloy* (Paris, 1951), p. 9. The possible significance of the change in translation will be discussed in Chapter VIII.

[2]I identify Worm with the character in the jar and Mahood with the traveler whose story was just mentioned above. This is not, however, the only possible way to read the book. William York Tindall, for example, identifies Mahood with both characters and interprets Worm as 'a kind of embryonic lump.' See Tindall, *Samuel Beckett*, pp. 31-32. The problem arises from the general vagueness of identity afflicting the Unnamable himself as well as his characters.

[3]This three-part schematic pattern was added to this passage in the English translation. In the French original there are only two outcries: *'Oui, crions, cette fois-ci, puis encore une peut-être'* (French text, p. 36). Perhaps, since the translation was done after the trilogy as a whole had taken shape, Beckett chose to add the third cry to fit the final structure of the trilogy.

[4]See Claude Mauriac, *L'Allitérature contemporaine* (Paris: Albin Michel, 1958), p. 85: *'Ces héros de livres en livres interchangeables sont tous des projections de l'auteur, qui est à l'image de nous-mêmes'* ('These heroes interchangeable from book to book are all projections of the author, who is himself the image of us').

CHAPTER VI

[1]See 'The Stages of Life,' in Carl Jung, *The Structure and Dynamics of the Psyche*, translation R. F. C. Hull (New York: Pantheon Books, 1960), pp. 387-403.

[2]The name Youdi may be a play on 'Dieu,' the French word for God. Similarly, the name Gaber may be an allusion to the archangel Gabriel, the messenger of God.

[3]As was mentioned in the chapter on *Watt*, the same allusion appears in reference to Watt's desire to see Mr Knott 'face to face' (*Watt*, p. 146).

[4]Compare Molloy here with Watt, for whom such endless calculations as 365 divided by seven (*Watt*, p. 34) were symbols of frustration.

[5]Compare Malone's desire for symmetry in the shape of his composition.

[6]Ruby Cohn in her article, 'Philosophical Fragments in the Works of Samuel Beckett,' cited above in Chapter II (note 3), has pointed out that this is an allusion to the following sentence from Geulincx's *Ethics*: *'Navis occissime vectorem abripiens versus occidentem, nihil impedit quominus ille in navi ipsa deambulet versus orientem'* ('Although the ship may be carrying him swiftly toward the west, nothing prevents a person in the ship from walking toward the east'). It is especially appropriate that in Molloy's adaptation the passenger is a slave on a ship captained by Ulysses, who, according to Dante's version of the story, was driven to his own destruction and that of his crew and ship by his irresistible desire *'a divenir del mondo esperto, /e delli vizi umani e del valore'* ('to gain experience of the world, /and of human vice and valor,' *Inferno XXVI*. 98-99). The ship of Ulysses was shipwrecked in the western ocean at the base of the mountain of purgatory. In Molloy's use of the image, the black ship sailing westward toward shipwreck is a symbol of the doom he expects from the compulsions that enslave him.

CHAPTER VII

[1]Beckett also uses imagery of light and darkness in many of his other works. Murphy divides his mind into light, half-light and dark; he prefers the dark (*Murphy*, pp. 111-13). Watt has a habitual aversion to light: see *Watt*, p. 33 and p. 153. Pozzo in *Waiting for Godot* (New York: Grove

Press, 1954) uses light to represent life and consciousness (*Godot*, p. 57a). In 'Endgame' (New York: Grove Press, 1958) light seems valuable since Hamm wants to sit in the light (p. 63) and since mother Pegg is said to have died 'of darkness' (p. 75). For Krapp in 'Krapp's Last Tape,' light seems to represent consciousness: he goes into the shadows to seek oblivion in darkness and comes into the light to listen to his tape recorder and think about his past. In 'Play' a beam of light, awaking the characters to consciousness, makes them think and speak.

[2]Imagery of birth into death is also used in *Waiting for Godot*, pp. 57a-58.

[3]See 'Play,' in which the three characters feel they have to speak of their sins in order to go silent.

CHAPTER VIII
[1]See *Proust*, p. 46, where Beckett speaks of 'that irremediable solitude to which every human being is condemned.'

[2]See Tindall, *Samuel Beckett*, p. 23.

[3]In *Proust*, p. 38, Beckett, paraphrasing Proust, refers to love as 'that desert of loneliness and recrimination.'

CHAPTER IX
[1]Quoted in Shenker, 'Moody Man of Letters,' pp. 1 and 3.

[2]Published in *Stories and Texts for nothing* (New York: Grove Press, 1967). All page references are to this edition.

[3]As the narrator thinks about home, he remembers a scene from his childhood in which his father told him a story about a Joe Breem, or Breen, son of a lighthouse keeper. This connects the narrator of this 'text' with the narrator of 'The Calmative' in *Stories*, whose father was said to have told him the same story.

[4]Quoted in Shenker, 'Moody Man of Letters,' p. 3.

[5]See Fletcher, *The Novels of Samuel Beckett*, p. 196.

[6]First published in French as *Comment c'est* (Paris: Éditions de Minuit, 1961) and later translated by the author as *How It Is* (New York: Grove Press, 1964). All English language references are to the Grove Press edition, all French language references to that of the Éditions de Minuit.

[7]Driver, 'Beckett by the Madeleine,' pp. 22-23.

CHAPTER X: *Postscript*
[1]All three of these works were published first in single editions by Éditions de Minuit, Paris. In 1967 they were reprinted in the collection *Têtes-Mortes* by the same publisher.

[2]London: Calder and Boyars, 1965. Reprinted in *No's Knife*, same publisher, 1967.

[3]In *No's Knife*.

[4]*Harper's Bazaar*, No. 3067 (June, 1967), pp. 120 and 140. And in *No's Knife*.

[5]*Biblio*, XXXV, No. 1 (January, 1967), 23-24.

[6]*Evergreen Review*, I, No. 1 (1957), 179-92. Reprinted in book form by Faber and Faber, London, 1958. Both narrators have memories of Bible-reading mothers, for example.

BIBLIOGRAPHY

This bibliography is in three sections. The first is a list in chronological order of the principal published works of Samuel Beckett. The second is a list of selected criticism. The third is a list of sources for biographical information. None of these pretends to be complete. The list of Beckett's works is limited to his more important imaginative writings and essays. The list of criticism is limited to works that would be useful to a person interested primarily in Beckett's novels. For further information in all three areas, the reader should see the critical bibliography, *Samuel Beckett: His Works and His Critics*, by Raymond Federman and John Fletcher (Berkeley and Los Angeles: University of California Press, 1970). There is also a more extensive list of criticism compiled by the present writer in *West Coast Review*, I, No. 1 (Spring, 1966), 56-70.

The Principal Published Works of Samuel Beckett in Chronological Order

'Assumption,' *Transition*, Nos. 16-17 (June, 1929), pp. 268-71. Reprinted in *Transition Workshop* (New York, 1949). Short story.

'Dante . . . Bruno. Vico . . Joyce.' Pp. 3-22 in *Our Exagmination Round His Factification for Incamination of Work in Progress*. Paris: Shakespeare and Co., 1929. Reprinted in *Transition*, Nos. 16-17 (June, 1929), pp. 242-53. *Our Exagmination* reissued in London by Faber and Faber (1936) and in New York by New Directions (1939 and 1962). Essay.

Whoroscope. Paris: Hours Press, 1930. Collected in *Poems in English*. London: Calder, 1961. New York: Grove Press, 1963. Poem.

Proust. London: Chatto and Windus, 1931. New York: Grove Press, 1957. London: Calder, 1958. Essay.

'Sedendo et Quiesciendo' [*sic*], *Transition*, No. 21 (March, 1932), pp. 13-20. Short story adapted from the unpublished 'Dream of Fair to Middling Women.'

'Dante and the Lobster,' *This Quarter* (December, 1932), pp. 222-36. Revised version included in *More Pricks than Kicks*, 1934. Short story.

More Pricks than Kicks. London: Chatto and Windus, 1934. Collection
of ten short stories: 'Dante and the Lobster,' 'Fingal,' 'Ding-Dong,' 'A
Wet Night,' 'Love and Lethe,' 'Walking Out,' 'What a Misfortune,'
'The Smeraldina's Billet-Doux,' 'Yellow,' and 'Draff.' 'Dante and the
Lobster' was reprinted in *Evergreen Review*, I, No. 1 (1957), 24-36.
'Yellow' was reprinted in *New World Writing*, No. 10 (New York:
Mentor, 1956), pp. 108-19.
'A Case in a Thousand,' *The Bookman*, London, LXXXVI, No. 515
(August, 1934), 241-42. Short story.
Echo's Bones and Other Precipitates. Paris: Europa Press, 1935. Collected
in *Samuel Beckett: Gedichte* (Wiesbaden: Limes Verlag, 1959) and in
Poems in English, 1961. Collection of poems.
'Cascando,' *Dublin Magazine*, XI, No. 4 (October-December, 1936), 3-4.
Collected in *Gedichte*, 1959, and in *Poems in English*, 1961. Poem.
Murphy. London: Routledge, 1938. New York: Grove Press, 1957. London:
Calder, 1963. Novel.
'Suite,' *Les Temps Modernes*, No. 10 (July, 1946), pp. 107-19. Revised
version entitled 'La Fin' in *Nouvelles et Textes pour rien*, 1955. Trans-
lated as 'The End' by Richard Seaver in collaboration with Samuel
Beckett, *Evergreen Review*, IV, No. 15 (1960), 22-41. Also in *Stories and
Texts for nothing* (New York: Grove Press, 1967). Short story.
'Poèmes 38-39,' *Les Temps Modernes*, No. 14 (November, 1946), pp. 288-
93. Collected in *Gedichte*, 1959. Set of twelve poems.
'L'Expulsé,' *Fontaine*, X, No. 57 (December, 1946–January, 1947), 685-708.
Revised version in *Nouvelles et Textes pour rien*, 1955. Translated as
'The Expelled' by Richard Seaver in collaboration with Samuel Beckett,
Evergreen Review, VI, No. 22 (January-February, 1962), 8-20. Also
in *Stories and Texts for nothing*, 1967. Short story.
Murphy, trans. Samuel Beckett. Paris: Bordas, 1947. Paris: Éditions de
Minuit, 1953. Translation into French.
'Three Poems' (in French and English versions) *Transition Forty-Eight*, No.
2 (June, 1948), pp. 96-97. Reprinted (English texts only) in *Poetry
Ireland*, No. 5 (April, 1949), and in *Gedichte*, 1959 (French texts only).
Molloy. Paris: Éditions de Minuit, 1951. Novel in French.
Malone meurt. Paris: Éditions de Minuit, 1951. Novel in French.
En Attendant Godot. Paris: Éditions de Minuit, 1952. Scholarly edition
annotated by Germain Brée and Eric Schoenfeld, published in New
York by Macmillan, 1963. Play in French.
L'Innommable. Paris: Éditions de Minuit, 1953. Novel in French.
Watt. Paris: Olympia Press, 1953 and 1958. New York: Grove Press,
1959. London: Calder, 1963. Novel in English.
Waiting for Godot, trans. Samuel Beckett. New York: Grove Press,
1954. London: Faber and Faber, 1956. Translation of *En Attendant
Godot*.
Nouvelles et Textes pour rien. Paris: Éditions de Minuit, 1955. There
are two sections: 'Nouvelles' and 'Textes pour rien.' In the 'Nouvelles'
section are the stories: L'Expulsé,' 'Le Calmant,' and 'La Fin.' 'Textes
pour rien' consists of thirteen texts. An editor's note says that the

'Nouvelles' date from 1945 and the 'Textes pour rien' from 1950.

'Trois Poèmes,' *Cahiers des Saisons,* No. 2 (October, 1955), pp. 115-16. Collected in *Gedichte,* 1959. Three poems in French.

Molloy, trans. from the French by Patrick Bowles in collaboration with Samuel Beckett. Paris: Olympia Press, 1955. New York: Grove Press, 1955. Collected in one-volume edition with *Malone Dies* and *The Unnamable* in 1959 by Grove Press (New York), Calder (London), and Olympia Press (Paris).

Malone Dies, trans. Samuel Beckett. New York: Grove Press, 1956. London: Calder, 1958. Translation of *Malone meurt.* Collected in one-volume edition with *Molloy* and *The Unnamable,* 1959.

'Fin de partie' (play in French) and 'Acte sans paroles' (mime). Published in one volume. Paris: Éditions de Minuit, 1957.

All That Fall. London: Faber and Faber, 1957. New York: Grove Press, 1957. Reprinted in *Krapp's Last Tape and Other Dramatic Pieces.* New York: Grove Press, 1960. Radio play.

Tous ceux qui tombent, trans. Robert Pinget and Samuel Beckett. Paris Éditions de Minuit, 1957. French translation of *All That Fall.*

'From an Abandoned Work,' *Evergreen Review,* I, No. 1 (1957), 179-92. Reprinted in book form by Faber and Faber, London, 1958. Prose fragment.

The Unnamable, trans. Samuel Beckett. New York: Grove Press, 1958. Collected in one volume with *Molloy* and *Malone Dies,* 1959. Translation of *L'Innommable.*

'Endgame' and 'Act without Words,' both translated by Samuel Beckett and published in one volume. New York: Grove Press, 1958. London: Faber and Faber, 1958. Translations of 'Fin de partie' and 'Actes sans paroles.'

'Krapp's Last Tape,' *Evergreen Review,* II, No. 5 (Summer, 1958), 13-24. Reprinted in *Krapp's Last Tape and Other Dramatic Pieces,* 1960. Play.

'Embers,' *Evergreen Review,* III, No. 10 (November-December, 1959), 24-41. Reprinted in *Krapp's Last Tape and Other Dramatic Pieces,* 1960. Radio play.

'La Dernière Bande' and 'Cendres.' Both published in one volume. 'La Dernière Bande' was translated by Pierre Leyris and Samuel Beckett, 'Cendres' by Robert Pinget and Samuel Beckett. Paris: Éditions de Minuit, 1959. Translations of 'Krapp's Last Tape' and 'Embers' into French.

'Text for nothing I,' trans. Samuel Beckett, *Evergreen Review,* III, No. 9 (Summer, 1959), 21-24. Also in *Stories and Texts for nothing,* 1967.

'Act without Words II,' translated from the French by Samuel Beckett, *New Departures,* No. 1 (Summer, 1959), pp. 89-91. Reprinted in *Krapp's Last Tape and Other Dramatic Pieces,* 1960. Mime.

'Madden and The Umbrella,' trans. Hugh Kenner and Raymond Federman, *Spectrum,* IV, No. 1 (Winter, 1960), 3-11. Excerpts from the unpublished novel, 'Mercier et Camier.'

Bram van Velde. Translated from the French by Samuel Beckett and Olive

Classe. New York: Grove Press, 1960. Essay.

Comment c'est. Paris: Éditions de Minuit, 1961. Novel in French.

Happy Days. New York: Grove Press, 1961. London: Faber and Faber, 1962. Play.

'Words and Music,' *Evergreen Review*, VI, No. 27 (November-December, 1962), 34-43. Radio play.

'Cascando,' translated from the French by Samuel Beckett, *Evergreen Review*, VII, No. 30 (May-June, 1963), 47-57. Radio play.

Oh les beaux jours, trans. Samuel Beckett. Paris: Éditions de Minuit, 1963. Translation of *Happy Days.*

'Play.' London: Faber and Faber, 1964. Play.

'Comédie,' trans. Samuel Beckett. *Lettres Nouvelles*, XII (June-July-August, 1964), 10-31. Translation of 'Play' into French.

How It Is, trans. Samuel Beckett. New York: Grove Press, 1964. London: Faber and Faber, 1964. Translation of *Comment c'est.*

'Imagination morte imaginez.' Paris: Éditions de Minuit, 1965. Short fiction.

'Imagination Dead Imagine,' trans. Samuel Beckett. London: Calder and Boyars, 1965. Translation of the above.

'Assez.' Paris: Éditions de Minuit, 1966. Short fiction.

'Bing.' Paris: Éditions de Minuit, 1966. Short fiction.

Comédie et Actes divers, trans. Samuel Beckett. Paris: Éditions de Minuit, 1966. Collection of theatrical pieces: 'Comédie,' 'Va et vient,' 'Cascando,' 'Paroles et musique,' 'Dis Joe,' 'Actes sans paroles II.'

'Dans le cylindre,' *Biblio*, XXXV, No. 1 (January, 1967), 23-24. Short fiction.

'Ping,' trans. Samuel Beckett, *Harper's Bazaar*, No. 3067 (June, 1967), pp. 120 and 140. Also in *No's Knife* (see below). Translation of 'Bing.'

Stories and Texts for nothing. Translations by Samuel Beckett except in the case of 'The Expelled' and 'The End,' which were translated by Richard Seaver in collaboration with Samuel Beckett. New York: Grove Press, 1967. Also in *No's Knife.* Translation of *Nouvelles et Textes pour rien.*

No's Knife. London: Calder and Boyars, 1967. Collection of fiction: 'The Expelled,' 'The Calmative,' 'The End,' 'Texts for nothing,' 'From an Abandoned Work,' 'Enough' (translation of 'Assez,' trans. Samuel Beckett), 'Imagination Dead Imagine,' 'Ping.'

Têtes-Mortes. Paris: Éditions de Minuit, 1967. Collection of fiction: 'D'un ouvrage abandonné' (translation of 'From an Abandoned Work,' translated by Ludovic and Agnes Janvier in collaboration with Samuel Beckett), 'Assez,' 'Imagination morte imaginez,' 'Bing.'

Come and Go: A Dramaticule. London: Calder and Boyars, 1967.

Selected Criticism

Abel, Lionel. 'Joyce the Father, Beckett the Son,' *New Leader*, XLII (December 14, 1959), 26-27.

Allsop, Kenneth. *The Angry Decade*. London: Peter Owen, 1958. Pp. 37-42.

Bataille, George. 'Le Silence de Molloy,' *Critique*, VII (May 15, 1951), 387-96.

Bowles, Patrick. 'How Samuel Beckett Sees the Universe,' *The Listener*, LIX (June 19, 1958), 10.

Benmussa, Simone. 'Samuel Beckett: essai de bibliographie,' *Biblio*, XXXV, No. 1 (January, 1967), 25-27.

Brée, Germaine. 'Beckett's Abstractors of Quintessence,' *French Review*, XXXVI (May, 1963), 567-76.

Coe, Richard N. 'God and Samuel Beckett,' *Meanjin Quarterly*, XXIV, No. 1 (1965), 66-85.

————. *Samuel Beckett*. New York: Grove Press, 1964.

Cohn, Ruby. 'A Note on Beckett, Dante, and Geulincx,' *Comparative Literature*, XII (Winter, 1960), 93-94.

————. 'Philosophical Fragments in the Works of Samuel Beckett,' *Criticism*, VI (Winter, 1964), 33-43. Reprinted in *Samuel Beckett: A Collection of Critical Essays*, ed. Martin Esslin.

————. *Samuel Beckett: The Comic Gamut*. New Brunswick, N. J.: Rutgers University Press, 1962.

————. '*Watt* in the Light of *The Castle*,' *Comparative Literature*, XIII (Spring, 1961), 154-66.

Esslin, Martin. 'Samuel Beckett,' chapter in *The Novelist as Philosopher: Studies in French Fiction, 1935-1960*, ed. John Cruikshank. London: Oxford University Press, 1962.

————, ed. *Samuel Beckett: A Collection of Critical Essays*. Englewood Cliffs, N. J.: Prentice-Hall, 1965.

Federman, Raymond. *Journey to Chaos: Samuel Beckett's Early Fiction*. Berkeley and Los Angeles: University of California Press, 1965.

Fletcher, John. 'Beckett et Proust,' *Caliban*, No. 1 (1964), pp. 89-100.

————. 'Beckett's Debt to Dante,' *Nottingham French Studies*, IV, No. 1 (1965), 41-52.

————. *The Novels of Samuel Beckett*. London: Chatto and Windus, 1964.

————. 'Samuel Beckett and the Philosophers,' *Comparative Literature*, XVII, No. 1 (Winter, 1965), 43-56.

Friedman, Melvin J. 'The Novels of Samuel Beckett: an Amalgam of Joyce
————. *Samuel Beckett's Art*. London: Chatto and Windus, 1967.
and Proust,' *Comparative Literature*, XII (Winter, 1960), 47-58.

————, ed. *Samuel Beckett*. Paris: Lettres Modernes, 1964. (Collection of essays in French by various authors.)

————. 'Samuel Beckett and the Nouveau Roman,' *Wisconsin Studies in Contemporary Literature*, I (Spring-Summer, 1960), 22-36.

Frye, Northrop. 'The Nightmare Life in Death,' *Hudson Review*, XIII (Autumn, 1960), 442-48.

Gessner, Niklaus. *Die Unzulänglichkeit der Sprache: Eine Untersuchung über Formzerfall und Beziehungslosigkeit bei Samuel Beckett*. Zurich: Juris Verlag, 1957.

Hayman, David. 'Quest for Meaninglessness: The Boundless Poverty of

Molloy,' in *Six Contemporary Novels,* ed. William O. S. Sutherland. Austin, Texas: University of Texas (Department of English), 1962. Pp. 90-112.

Hesla, David H. 'The Shape of Chaos: A Reading of Beckett's *Watt,*' *Critique,* VI, No. 1 (Spring, 1963), 85-105.

Hoefer, Jacqueline. '*Watt,*' *Perspective,* XI (Autumn, 1959), 166-82. Reprinted in *Samuel Beckett: A Collection of Critical Essays,* ed. Martin Esslin.

Hoffman, Frederick J. 'L'Insaisissable moi: Les 'M' de Beckett,' *Revue des Lettres Modernes,* No. 100 (1964), pp. 23-53.

———. *Samuel Beckett: The Language of Self.* Carbondale: Southern Illinois University Press, 1962.

Jacobsen, Josephine, and William R. Mueller. *The Testament of Samuel Beckett.* New York: Hill and Wang, 1964.

Janvier, Ludovic. *Pour Samuel Beckett.* Paris: Éditions de Minuit, 1966.

Kenner, Hugh. *Samuel Beckett: A Critical Study.* New York: Grove Press, 1961.

Kermode, Frank. 'Beckett, Snow, and Pure Poverty,' *Encounter,* XV (July, 1960), 73-76.

Kern, Edith. 'Moran-Molloy: The Hero as Author,' *Perspective,* XI (Autumn, 1959), 183-92.

Loy, J. Robert. '*Things* in Recent French Literature,' *PMLA,* LXXI (March, 1956), 27-41.

Mauriac, Claude. *L'Allitérature contemporaine.* Paris: Albin Michel, 1958. English translation, *The New Literature,* trans. Samuel I. Stone. New York: George Braziller, 1959.

Mercier, Vivian. *The Irish Comic Tradition.* London: Oxford University Press, 1962.

———. 'The Mathematical Limit,' *Nation,* CLXXXVIII (February 14, 1959), 144-45.

Micha, René. 'Une Nouvelle Littérature Allégorique,' *Nouvelle Nouvelle Revue Française,* II (April, 1954), 696-706.

Mintz, Samuel I. 'Beckett's *Murphy:* A "Cartesian" Novel,' *Perspective,* IX (Autumn, 1959), 156-65.

Montgomery, Niall. 'No Symbols Where None Intended,' *New World Writing,* No. 5 (New York: Mentor, 1954). Pp. 324-37.

Scott, Nathan A., Jr. *Samuel Beckett.* London: Bowes and Bowes, 1965.

Senneff, Susan Field. 'Song and Music in Samuel Beckett's *Watt,*' *Modern Fiction Studies,* X (Summer, 1964), 137-49.

Strauss, Walter A. 'Dante's Belacqua and Beckett's Tramps,' *Comparative Literature,* XI (Summer, 1959), 250-61.

Tindall, William York. 'Beckett's Bums,' *Critique,* II (Spring-Summer, 1958).

———. *Samuel Beckett.* New York: Columbia University Press, 1964.

Warhaft, Sidney. 'Threne and Theme in *Watt,*' *Wisconsin Studies in Contemporary Literature,* IV (Autumn, 1963), 261-78.

Wellershoff, Dieter. 'Failure of an Attempt at De-Mythologization: Samuel

Beckett's Novels,' in *Samuel Beckett: A Collection of Critical Essays*, ed. Martin Esslin.

Biographical Material, Interviews, and Impressions of Beckett as a Person

Anonymous. 'Messenger of Gloom,' *The Observer* (November 9, 1958).

Aubarede, Gabriel d'. 'En attendant . . . Beckett,' *Nouvelles Littéraires* (February 16, 1961), pp. 1 and 7. Reprinted in English under the title, 'Waiting for Beckett,' *Trace*, No. 42 (Summer, 1961), pp. 156-58.

Bowles, Patrick. Translator's Foreword to *The Visit* by Friedrich Dürenmatt. New York: Grove Press, 1962.

Driver, Tom F. 'Beckett by the Madeleine,' *Columbia University Forum*, IV, No. 3 (Summer, 1961), 21-25.

Ellmann, Richard. *James Joyce*. New York: Oxford University Press, 1959.

Gilbert, Stuart, ed. *Letters of James Joyce*. New York: Viking Press, 1957.

Gorman, Herbert. *James Joyce*. New York: B. W. Huebsch, 1924.

Guggenheim, Marguerite. *Out of This Century*. New York: Dial Press, 1946.

————. *Confessions of an Art Addict*. New York: Macmillan, 1960.

Say, A. de. 'Rousillon,' *L'Arc*, II (Spring, 1958), p. 83.

Schneider, Alain. 'Waiting for Beckett: A Personal Chronicle,' *Chelsea Review*, II (Autumn, 1958), 3-20.

Shenker, Israel. 'Moody Man of Letters,' New York *Times*, CV (Sunday, May 6, 1956), Section 2, pp. 1 and 3.

INDEX

A and B (French version of *Molloy*),
   139
A and C (*Molloy*), 72, 83, 139, 140
Abbey Theatre, Dublin, 50
Abel. *See* Christian imagery
Absurd, the: as a cultural concept,
   29-30, 168
Absurdity: as theme in *Watt*, 17
A la recherche du temps perdu
   (Proust), 29, 30
Alexander of Hales, 59
Ambrose, Father (*Molloy*), 97, 102,
   142
Analogy, as principle in theology:
   Watt, 60; *Molloy*, 101
Anna Livia Plurabelle (Joyce):
   Beckett as translator of, 15
Antepurgatory, Dante's, 23, 44-45,
   46
Aquinas, Saint Thomas, 22, 25
Archetypal patterns: *Watt*, 56-57;
   trilogy, 86-87
Aristotle, 26-27
Arsene (*Watt*), 61-63, 67-68
'Assez.' *See* 'Enough'
'Assumption,' 31-32
Astrology: in *Murphy*, 46, 52-53
Attachment, theme of. *See* Desire
Authors, Beckett's characters as, 30

Basil (*The Unnamable*), 80
Beatrice, Dante's, 45-46
Beckett, Samuel Barclay: biographical data, 15, 21; attitude toward
   philosophy, 19, 21; academic
   background, 21-22, 26, 28; not

a Cartesian, 27-28; as the true
   narrator of the trilogy, 86. *See
   also* Technique
Belacqua, Dante's, 23, 44-45
'Belacqua bliss,' 23, 44-45
Belacqua Shuah (*More Pricks than
   Kicks*): name derived from Dante,
   23; indolence, 33-34, 37; desire
   for isolation, 33-34; sexual tastes,
   33-34; need for fellowship, 34-35;
   physical impairments, 35; need to
   keep moving, 35-37; solipsism, 35;
   pursued by Furies, 35; attracted
   by insanity, 37; desire to return
   to womb, 37; feelings about death,
   37-39; unconcerned with politics,
   39; concern with justice of God,
   39-40; attitude toward Dante, 39-
   41; self-deception, 40-41; pose of
   self-sufficiency, 41; implicit Cartesianism, 41; narrator's critical
   attitude toward, 41-42
Bem (*How It Is*), 159-60
Bicycles: in *More Pricks than Kicks*,
   33; in *Molloy*, 95
'Bing.' *See* 'Ping'
Birth, as image; in *Malone Dies*,
   124-25; in *The Unnamable*, 125-
   27
Bom (*How It Is*), 159-60
Bonaventura, Saint, 59
Buddhism, 52

'Calmant, Le.' See *Stories*
'Calmative, The.' See *Stories*

185